Technological Change and
Productivity Growth

FUNDAMENTALS OF PURE AND APPLIED ECONOMICS

EDITORS-IN-CHIEF

J. LESOURNE, Conservatoire National des Arts et Métiers, Paris, France
H. SONNENSCHEIN, Princeton University, Princeton, NJ, USA

ADVISORY BOARD

K. ARROW, Stanford, CA, USA
W. BAUMOL, Princeton, NJ, USA
W. A. LEWIS, Princeton, NJ, USA
S. TSURU, Tokyo, Japan

SECTIONS AND EDITORS

BALANCE OF PAYMENTS AND INTERNATIONAL FINANCE
W. Branson, Princeton University

DISTRIBUTION
A. Atkinson, London School of Economics

ECONOMIC DEMOGRAPHY
T.P. Schultz, Yale University

ECONOMIC DEVELOPMENT STUDIES
S. Chakravarty, Delhi School of Economics

ECONOMIC FLUCTUATIONS: FORECASTING, STABILIZATION, INFLATION, SHORT TERM MODELS, UNEMPLOYMENT
A. Ando, University of Pennsylvania

ECONOMIC HISTORY
P. David, Stanford University, and M. Lévy-Leboyer, Université Paris X

ECONOMIC SYSTEMS
J.M. Montias, Yale University, and J. Kornai, Institute of Economics, Hungarian Academy of Sciences

ECONOMICS OF HEALTH, EDUCATION, POVERTY AND CRIME
V. Fuchs, Stanford University

ECONOMICS OF THE HOUSEHOLD AND INDIVIDUAL BEHAVIOR
J. Muellbauer, University of Oxford

ECONOMICS OF TECHNOLOGICAL CHANGE
F. M. Scherer, Swarthmore College

ECONOMICS OF UNCERTAINTY AND INFORMATION
S. Grossman, Princeton University, and J. Stiglitz, Princeton University

Continued on inside back cover

Technological Change and Productivity Growth

Albert N. Link
University of North Carolina at Greensboro, USA

A volume in the Economics of Technological Change section

edited by

F. M. Scherer
Swarthmore College, USA

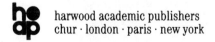

harwood academic publishers
chur · london · paris · new york

© 1987 by Harwood Academic Publishers GmbH
Poststrasse 22, 7000 Chur, Switzerland

Harwood Academic Publishers

Post Office Box 197
London WC2E 9PX
England

58, rue Lhomond
75005 Paris
France

Post Office Box 786
Cooper Station
New York, NY 10276
United States of America

Library of Congress Cataloging-in-Publication Data

Link, Albert N.
  Technological change and productivity growth.

  (Fundamentals of pure and applied economics; vol. 13.
Economics of technological change section, ISSN 0191-1708)
  Bibliography: p.
  Includes index.
  1. Technological innovations—Economic aspects.
2. Industrial productivity. I. Title. II. Series:
Fundamentals of pure and applied economics; vol. 13.
III. Series: Fundamentals of pure and applied
economics. Economics of technological change section.
HC79.T4L56 1986   338'.06   86-15031
ISBN 3-7186-0347-0

Contents

Introduction to the Series

Drawing on a personal network, an economist can still relatively easily stay well informed in the narrow field in which he works, but to keep up with the development of economics as a whole is a much more formidable challenge. Economists are confronted with difficulties associated with the rapid development of their discipline. There is a risk of "balkanisation" in economics, which may not be favorable to its development.

Fundamentals of Pure and Applied Economics has been created to meet this problem. The discipline of economics has been subdivided into sections (listed inside). These sections include short books, each surveying the state of the art in a given area.

Each book starts with the basic elements and goes as far as the most advanced results. Each should be useful to professors needing material for lectures, to graduate students looking for a global view of a particular subject, to professional economists wishing to keep up with the development of their science, and to researchers seeking convenient information on questions that incidentally appear in their work.

Each book is thus a presentation of the state of the art in a particular field rather than a step-by-step analysis of the development of the literature. Each is a high-level presentation but accessible to anyone with a solid background in economics, whether engaged in business, government, international organizations, teaching, or research in related fields.

Three aspects of *Fundamentals of Pure and Applied Economics* should be emphasized:

—First, the project covers the whole field of economics, not only theoretical or mathematical economics.

—Second, the project is open-ended and the number of books is not predetermined. If new interesting areas appear, they will generate additional books.

—Last, all the books making up each section will later be grouped to constitute one or several volumes of an Encyclopedia of Economics.

The editors of the sections are outstanding economists who have selected as authors for the series some of the finest specialists in the world.

J. Lesourne   *H. Sonnenschein*

Technological Change and Productivity Growth†

ALBERT N. LINK

University of North Carolina at Greensboro, USA

1. INTRODUCTION

Productivity growth is vital to economic well-being because it enhances standards of living and the quality of life. It improves production efficiency, which in turn enhances the competitive, financial and military position of a nation within the international community. It increases income, which potentially then can be reallocated toward improving conditions of social concern such as environmental pollution or poverty, and thereby enhancing quality of life. Productivity advances ameliorate inflationary pressures and thereby help establish economic stability. And, productivity growth stimulates market competition within an economy and between economies, thus improving resource allocation in general.

One thing responsible for productivity growth is technological change, or technical progress. Technological change brings about production efficiencies, which in turn lead to productivity growth. To understand the concept of productivity growth better, both for academic as well as policy-related concerns, it is imperative also to understand the nature of technological change and the linkages between the two dynamics.

The importance of technical progress and economic growth has long been known to students of economics. Traditionally, scholars

† Sincere thanks go to Mike Scherer, Barry Hirsch, Dave Kemme, Knox Lovell, John Lunn, Greg Tassey, and Eleanor Thomas for their useful comments and suggestions on earlier drafts of this paper.

1

refer to the first chapter in Adam Smith's *An Inquiry into the Nature and Causes of the Wealth of Nations* [315] in order to motivate a discussion of the technology-growth relationship.[1] This is a useful starting point. However, insights into this subject can be gleaned from the writings of even earlier scholars—the physiocrats. For example, Baudeau's [20] view was that the sources of economic growth fall into two categories: those that are subject to human control and thereby depend on knowledge and ability, and those that do not. It was Baudeau's entrepreneur who exercised intelligence in combining ideas in order to bring about innovations, and thereby to influence economic growth.

Contemporary interest in these topics was spurred as a result of several empirical studies during the 1950s which concluded that technological change was the most important single factor associated with aggregate economic growth. Partly as a result of these studies, which are discussed below, a body of literature began to grow. Its focus was on the technology-to-productivity growth relationship, the economics of growth itself, and the microfoundations of technological change.[2] In the 1970s, the apparent retardation of productivity growth in most industrialized nations revived the interest of scholars in these topics. The purpose of this paper is to survey the body of literature related to technological change and productivity growth.

The nine remaining sections trace the development of thought on these lines. First, in Section 2 some preliminary concepts are presented to give different viewpoints a common frame of reference. Then, in Section 3, a very brief review of the early economic studies on productivity growth is presented. These works have already been surveyed in an annotated fashion by Nadiri [235] and Kennedy and Thirlwall [175]. They are briefly referenced here only to set the stage.

Section 4 presents an overview of the production function

---

[1] For Smith, "innovation" is the product of division of labor, which in turn depends on the extent of the market, and it is innovation which leads to economic growth. Smith's innovator, his "philosopher" or "speculator," was an amateur by our modern standards. But Smith's view of innovation as a professional activity was indeed ahead of its time.

[2] A review of the economics literature on growth theory is beyond the bounds of this paper. Two excellent surveys have been written by Hahn and Matthews [137] and by Solow [322].

approach to conceptualizing and measuring technological change. Other useful frameworks are discussed in Section 5. Again, an excellent review of this literature already exists in [31], and therefore the literature is only summarized.

A summary of the facts about productivity growth trends in both the U.S. and in other industrialized countries is in Section 6. Section 7 offers a synthesis of the myriad factors commonly thought to contribute to productivity growth trends.

A conceptual model of sources of technological change is posited in Section 8; the empirical evidence in its support is reviewed, in an annotated fashion, in Section 9.

Finally, some summary remarks conclude the paper in Section 10.

2. SOME PRELIMINARY CONCEPTS

2.1. Productivity and productivity growth

There is no single generally accepted way to measure productivity or productivity growth. The more common measures begin with a production function representation of the input-to-output transformation process. The concept of a production function is not viewed by all as a valid point of departure. Nevertheless, given this conceptualization, productivity may be thought of as the degree of efficiency exhibited in the process of turning inputs into output. More specifically, total factor productivity describes the ratio of output to the combination of all inputs used. Partial factor productivity measures a ratio of output to the amount used of one single input (usually labor).

If output, Q, and a vector of n inputs $(x_1, \ldots ,x_n)$, denoted by X, are related as

$$Q = A(t)f(X), \qquad (1)$$

where $A(t)$ is a time-related shift factor, then total factor productivity, TFP, (a concept first introduced by Tinbergen [343] and Stigler [325]) can be approximated as

$$\text{TFP} = A(t) = Q/f(X) = Q/\Sigma\ w_i x_i, \qquad (2)$$

where the w_is$(0 \le w_i \le 1)$ are the individual input weights. Partial factor productivity can be written as Q/x_i.

Technological change may refer to the percentage rate of growth over time of total factor productivity, and is denoted as

$$\frac{\dot{TFP}}{TFP} = \frac{\dot{A}(t)}{A(t)} = \frac{\dot{A}}{A},\tag{3}$$

where the "dot" notation refers to a time derivative, and where the time notation on $A(t)$ frequently is dropped for simplicity.

2.2. Technology and technological change

Researchers have used the concept of technology in a variety of ways. In a narrow sense, technology refers to specific physical tools, but in a broader sense it describes whole social processes (i.e., intangible tools). Although there are analytical advantages to both the narrow and the more encompassing views, the different usages of the concept invariably promote confusion at both the theoretical and empirical levels.

A concept of technology that embraces social or intangible entities is eschewed in this paper. Although important, concepts like "technological ethic" and "organizational technology" are not directly related to the work reviewed below. Instead, the focus here is on the more narrow view of technology (although this does not remove all of the problems). In focusing on physical technology, questions arise such as: How can technologies be differentiated? and, What aspects of technology are of interest? Economists have attempted to answer these and related questions by implicitly dealing with the indirectly perceivable aspects of physical "tools," namely, the knowledge embedded within the technology.

Conceptualizing technology as the physical representation of knowledge provides a useful foundation for understanding technological change and its determinants.[3] Any useful technological device is, in part, proof of the knowledge-based or informational assumptions leading to its creation. The information embodied in a technology varies according to its source, type, and application. For

---

[3] Several writers have been careful to define their starting concepts. For example, Rosegger's [279] definition of technology as human knowledge applied in production is appropriate. Also, Freeman [106, 107] begins with a knowledge-based view of technology. For a limited review of such definitions see Tornatzky [344].

example, one source of information is science, although scientific knowledge is rarely sufficient for the more particular needs entailed in constructing (literally) a technological device.[4] Other sources of knowledge include information from controlled experimentation, information from trial and error, information of the kind philosophers refer to as "ordinary knowledge," and finally, information of the kind that falls under the rubrics of creativity, perceptiveness, and inspiration.[5]

This informational view of technology implies that technology *per se* is an output from a consciously undertaken process. Such an idea highlights the role of research in the generation of technologies. Starting there, technologies can be distinguished, albeit imperfectly, by the amount of embedded information. More concretely, research and development (R&D) activities play a large role in creating a new technology.

Closely related to the concept of technology is the notion of invention and innovation. One useful distinction is to associate "newness" with invention and "usefulness" (that is, putting an invention into practice) with innovation. But even at this general level, there remains a terminological problem: Does "new" refer to something new in the world, or to something new to the user [277, 361]? Mohr [229] defines an invention as something new brought into being, whereas an innovation is something new brought into use. The characteristic of newness appears in the writings of most scholars who address this topic. For example, Kuznets [185, p. 19] refers to inventive activity as a "new combination of available knowledge." Rosegger [279] and Sato and Suzawa [294] also stress this idea.

For the purposes at hand, it is helpful to think of an invention as

---

[4] It may be useful in this regard to think of science as focusing on the understanding of knowledge and technology as focusing on the application of knowledge.

[5] Machlup [208, p. 182] argues that formal education is only one form of knowledge; knowledge is also gained experientially, and at different rates by different individuals. Individuals can accrue knowledge from their day-to-day experiences:

Some alert and quick-minded persons, by keeping their eyes and ears open for new facts and theories, discoveries and opportunities, perceive what normal people, of lesser alertness and perceptiveness, would fail to notice. Hence, new knowledge is available at little or no cost to those who are on the lookout . . ..

the creation of a new technology, or the new use of an existing technology.[6] Innovation, then, is the first application of the invention (a technology) in production.[7] Since innovation (application) implies the beginning of a diffusion process, this conceptualization parallels the Schumpeterian idea that there are phases in the process of technological change: invention, innovation and diffusion (imitation). Along similar lines, Usher [345] posited that technology is the result of an innovation, and an innovation is the result of an invention (which results as the emergence of "new things" requiring an "act of insight" going beyond the normal exercise of technical or professional skills).

3. EARLY STUDIES ON PRODUCTIVITY GROWTH: AN OVERVIEW

Formal theories of the relationship between technological change and productivity growth were developed primarily during the 1970s. However, early post-World War II researchers perceived the generic importance of technological change as an underlying force for growth.[8] As Nelson [246, p. 1030] observes, these early writers "are remarkable in foreshadowing the central conclusion of studies done somewhat later within the neoclassical framework."

Schmookler [306], Mills [227], Schultz [308], Leontief [188], Fabricant [96], Valavanis-Vail [348] and Kendrick [164] found that aggregate growth over time had been due only in part to resource growth.[9] The average annual rates of productivity growth reported in Table I estimate increases in output, holding the quantity of inputs fixed, that is, increases in resource efficiency. Presumably, these efficiency gains were in part the result of some technological

---

[6] This view encompasses the views of those who treat an invention as simply a "blueprint" as well as those who see it as "new advances in knowledge" (and the two views need not be mutually exclusive).

[7] Scherer's [297] study of the Watt–Boulton steam-engine venture supports this relationship between invention and innovation in the process of technological change. Ruttan [283], however, disputes the necessity of the chronology. See Schumpeter [310, 311].

[8] These early studies are mentioned here primarily to set the stage for the later works in this area. More complete reviews of the early studies already exist. For example, see Nadiri [235] or Kennedy and Thirlwall [175].

[9] Leontief [188] used input-output analysis, rather than the traditionally used productivity indices, to arrive at his conclusions.

TABLE I

Technological change-economic growth relationship from early studies of
the U.S. economy

Researcher	Average annual rate of change
Schmookler [306]	
1869–78 to 1929–38	
G.N.P. per unit of input	1.36 percent
Mills [227]	
1891–1900 to 1941–50	
G.N.P. per manhour	3.6 percent
Schultz [308]	
1910 to 1950	
Agricultural output per unit	
of input	0.8 percent to 1.35 percent
Kendrick [164]	
1899 to 1953	
Private domestic output per unit	
of input	1.7 percent
Solow [318]	
1909 to 1949	
G.N.P. per unit of labor	1.5 percent

advances. In addition, Schmookler [p. 225] pointed out that his estimates "controvert the time-honored belief in a continuous increase in rate of technical progress," thus suggesting that there have been long innovation cycles characterizing technological growth patterns over time.

Abramovitz [1] examined economic activity in the post-Civil war economy, 1869–78 to 1944–53. He cautiously concluded that the source of growth in output per unit of labor over that time period was not increased resources per head. Rather, it rested within the realm of such a little understood cause as the growth in the stock of knowledge. It is no wonder, then, that Abramovitz coined the descriptive phrase, "measure of our ignorance," when referring to the determinants of productivity growth. He did conjecture that the inputs into this stock of knowledge were such factors as research and education.

Solow [318] was the first to formalize the study of productivity growth within the context of an aggregate production function model. His empirical analysis, applied to the U.S. economy for the period 1909 to 1949, led him to conclude, like earlier writers, that [p. 320] "gross output per man-hour doubled over the [time] interval, with $87\frac{1}{2}$ percent of the increase attributable to technical change. . . ." Solow recognized that his conclusion compared closely with that of Fabricant [96], who estimated that about 90 percent of the increase in output per capita between 1871 and 1951 was attributable to technical progress, as well as with the conclusions of Schmookler [306] and Valavanis-Vail [348].

The research that followed from these early studies had a dual focus. First, it was concerned with understanding and refining the aggregate production function model posited by Solow, thereby attempting to measure more accurately technological change and its economic consequences. And second, it was concerned with improving input measures used to calculate productivity indices.

4. THE PRODUCTION FUNCTION CONCEPT OF TECHNOLOGICAL CHANGE

4.1. Classification schemes

One method of evaluating the effect of technological change on production is in terms of changes in the amount of capital and labor (assuming only two factors of production) used in production. The simplest scheme assumes that technological change alters the input mix for a fixed level of output. For a given level of output and input price ratio, a labor-saving technological change results in a higher capital-to-labor ratio; a capital-saving technological change in a lower capital-to-labor ratio; and a neutral technological change in an unchanged capital-to-labor ratio. In terms of Figure 1, a labor-saving technological change results in isoquant I (output level Q^*) shifting inward to point A, whereas a capital-saving change results in a shift to point B. A neutral technological change is shown by a parallel shift in isoquant I inward to point C. At point C, Q^* is produced with proportionally less capital and less labor.[10]

---

[10] This conceptualization implicitly assumes that technology leads to cost-reducing changes rather than new or improved consumer products. Very roughly, this distinction corresponds to one between "process" and "product" improvements. (The correspondence is not perfect because product improvements in capital goods can be cost-reducing for the purchasers.) The distinction between process and product innovations can be traced at least to Ricardo and Mill; a more contemporary review is in Blaug [31]. The process/product distinction is especially important when characterizing research activity and evaluating its impact on productivity growth.

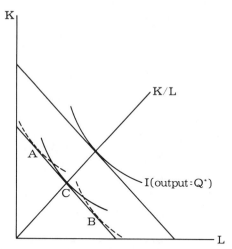

FIGURE 1   Labor-saving, capital-saving and neutral technological change: output held constant.

This scheme is most applicable at the microeconomic (firm or industry) level with a focus on the short-run, that is, when output levels can meaningfully be thought to remain constant. The scheme represents an unrealistic starting point for a macroeconomic taxonomy. However, three alternative long-run macroeconomic classification schemes have been suggested by Hicks [146] and Robinson [273], Harrod [139], and Solow [321] based upon a constant capital-to-labor, constant capital-to-output and constant labor-to-output ratio, respectively.[11]

Hicksian technological change ("innovation") is defined to be labor-saving, capital-saving or neutral if it raises, lowers or leaves unchanged the marginal product of capital relative to the marginal product of labor for a given capital-to-labor ratio.[12] In terms of Figure 2, if isoquant I characterizes production initially, then isoquant II reflects a labor-saving technological change, isoquant III

---

[11] Robinson's classification scheme is identical to the Hicksian scheme except that it is postulated in terms of average rather than marginal products.

[12] The slope of a linear isocost curve is the ratio of the price of labor to the price of capital. For a profit maximizing firm whose isoquant is tangent to its isocost curve, as in Figure 2, the ratio of input prices equals the ratio of the marginal products of the inputs.

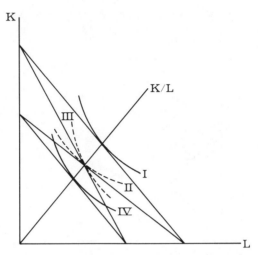

FIGURE 2　Labor-saving, capital-saving and neutral technological change: capital-to-labor ratio held constant.

a capital-saving technological change, and isoquant IV a neutral technological change.[13]

More formally, if the production function originally written in Eq. (1) is represented in a more general form as

$$Q = f(K, L; t),\qquad(4)$$

where the function $f(K, L; t)$ is linearly homogeneous and twice differentiable:

$$f_K, f_L > 0;\qquad f_{KK}, f_{LL} < 0;\qquad(5)$$

then, following Nadiri's [235] exposition, disembodied (independent of factor inputs) technological change is Hicks labor-saving, neutral or captial-savings as:

$$\left.\frac{\delta(f_K/K/f_L/L)}{\delta t}\right|_{K/L} \gtreqless 0.\qquad(6)$$

Alternatively formulated [in 82, 98, 101], technological change is

---

[13] Blaug [31] correctly notes that this Hicksian scheme conceptualizes the *initial* impact of the technology adoption of the production process, that is, when input supplies remain constant. This is not the case in the Harrod [139] or Solow [321] schemes.

Hicks labor-saving, neutral or capital-saving as the technological bias, B, is

$$B = \left[\frac{\delta f_K / \delta t}{f_K} - \frac{\delta f_L / \delta t}{f_L} \right] \gtreqless 0. \qquad (7)$$

Hicks [146, pp. 124–125] first introduced the idea that technological bias is inherent within (endogenous to) an economic system. He wrote that a "change in the relative prices of the factors of production is itself a spur to economizing the use of a factor which has become relatively expensive." Although disputed by Salter [287], who argued that firms seek *total* cost reduction rather than single factor savings, the endogeneity of factor bias has been stressed repeatedly by Brozen [41], Fellner [99], Kennedy [174], Samuelson [288], von Weizsäcker [350], Drandakis and Phelps [88], Ahmad [5], and McCain [223], among others.[14]

Referring again to Eq. (4) technological change is Harrod labor-saving, neutral or capital-saving as

$$\frac{\delta (f_K / K / f_L / L)}{\delta t} \bigg|_{K/Q} \gtreqless 0. \qquad (8)$$

Likewise, technological change is Solow labor-saving, neutral or capital-saving as

$$\frac{\delta (f_K / K / f_L / L)}{\delta t} \bigg|_{L/Q} \gtreqless 0. \qquad (9)$$

These classification schemes are useful theoretical constructs for thinking about the impact of technological change on production. Their descriptive usefulness is subject to empirical verification. Efforts toward this end are discussed below.

4.2. Production function based measures of productivity

4.2a. The aggregate production function

Partial factor and total factor productivity estimates are formulated on the implicit assumption that a production function accurately

---

[14] For a review of these theoretical models see Nadiri [235] or Ferguson [101].

describes the maximum output attainable from a set of factor inputs. This production process is inherently microeconomic in nature. Questions arise regarding its meaning when applied at the aggregate level (at which most empirical calculations are made).[15] To see this, consider a more rigorous treatment of Eq. (1) and the underlying assumptions.

To derive Eq. (1), one begins with a generalized multi-input and multi-output production function written as

$$H(Q_{1t}, \ldots, Q_{mt}; X_{1t} \ldots X_{nt}; t) = H(\tilde{Q}; \tilde{X}; t) = 0, \qquad (10)$$

where the symbol $\sim$ denotes the vectors of m-numbered outputs (Qs) and n-numbered inputs (Xs).[16] If the function H is homothetic and weakly separable as defined by H^*, then, by definition, one can write it as

$$H(\tilde{Q}; \tilde{X}; t) = H^*(G^*(\tilde{Q}); F^*(\tilde{X}); t) = 0; \qquad (11)$$

and if the separability of the function is additive, then

$$G(\tilde{Q}) = F(\tilde{X}; t). \qquad (12)$$

Finally, if the multi-output vector is replaced by a single "composite output" vector Q, and if time-related technology is Hicks neutral and disembodied, then Eq. (12) becomes

$$Q = A(t)f(X), \qquad (13)$$

which is identical to Eq. (1).[17]

At the aggregate level, the assumption of separability is questionable. Sudit and Finger [329, p. 8], for example, contend that the assumption is "economically restrictive since most production processes . . . probably do not in general exhibit independence of input and output substitution rates along the efficiency frontiers." Among others, Afriat [3] expresses similar concern. Gold [117] objects to the production function concept in general, arguing that

---

[15] A review of the literature regarding the nature and appropriateness of an aggregate production function specification is beyond the scope of this paper. The early debate is formulated in Robinson [274, 275], Champernowne [48] and Solow [317]. An excellent overview of the arguments is in Harcourt [138] or Blaug [32].

[16] This derivation comes from Berndt [24] and Sudit and Finger [329].

[17] See Diewert [84] for a more complete discussion of the necessary conditions to represent output by a composite index Q. The derivations that follow are based on a composite output index Q; however, this is only a simplification. Duality theory accommodates productivity growth estimates in a multi-output framework.

it is inherently impossible to measure the physical efficiency of any production process. Finally, the implicit assumption of production efficiency (or more precisely, the assumption that firms know all efficient input combinations, whether they have been tried or not), which underlies Eqs. (1) and (13), is likewise said to be unrealistic by Farrell [97].

In addition to these concerns, the parameter $A(t)$ is a potential source for measurement error. It reflects only one aspect of the production-related effects of technological change. $A(t)$ is a *shift* factor, and as such it does not measure movements *along* the production function. As a result, any comparison of productivity indices between points in time implicitly assumes either that all inputs (including management) are efficiently utilized at the production surface [6], or that the extent of inefficiency (input or organizational) is constant over time [250].

Nelson and Winter [247] motivate their evolutionary model of growth in part from their dissatisfaction with certain asserted shortcomings in the neoclassical model. The latter model implies that there is no room for entrepreneurial activity or innovational search in the production process. In the neoclassical tradition, technical knowledge is a pure public good—firms can select in a profit-maximizing way from all known (tried or untried) technical possibilities to produce their output, and nothing is assumed to be unknown. Although the Nelson–Winter evolutionary models do not offer an alternative to total factor productivity measurement (in fact, they define it away), they do offer an important framework for questioning the logic behind approximating technological change by changes in a time-related shift factor.

The criticisms noted here are not without merit. Still, apart from data problems, the production function approach appears to have considerable construct validity. For example, Nadiri [235, p. 1146] writes that "the use of an aggregate production function gives reasonably good estimates ... due mainly to the narrow range of movement of aggregate data rather than the solid foundation of the function."

4.2b. Partial factor productivity indices

Labor (L) productivity indices, the most commonly used partial factor productivity measure, have been "popular" for decades, partly because of their ease of calculation. However, this advantage is not without its cost. For example, the use of Q/L, or the average product of labor, as a measure of productivity has "numerous serious, if not quite fatal conceptual flaws" [259, p. 116]. Even so, labor productivity indices still remain widely used. According to Christainsen and Haveman [51, p. 3]: "although [these] productivity measures . . . have serious weaknesses, the picture of productivity change which they yield is not greatly different from that of more complete measures." Three of these "flaws" are as follows.

First, to ensure reliability, output and input measures must be consistent, that is, they must refer to the same production activity. Since there are many production activities implicitly underlying any aggregate measure of output, a meaningful composite measure must be formed by denominating the value of each output measure by an appropriate price index. However, when labor is denominated in hours, conceptual problems arise because a labor hours measure corrects for only one of the many heterogeneous aspects of workers, namely the number of hours each works. Additional adjustments are needed. The age/sex/skill composition of the labor force varies over time and from sector to sector. Since average labor productivity indices are primarily used for intertemporal comparisons, changes in the composition of the work force will affect measured Q, but will not be reflected accurately in a Q/L index unless the changes are perfectly correlated with the way L is measured. This conceptual problem can be overcome by adjusting L for the heterogeneity of the labor force [73, 184, 224]. Perloff and Wachter [259] refer to such an improved index, written in terms of efficiency labor units, as a "demographically adjusted measure of productivity."

Baumol and Wolff [21] observe that there are several ways to aggregate over heterogeneous outputs (used in either partial or total factor productivity indices). A "base year" approach adjusts output values by the price of each product in the base period. The "deflated price" approach adjusts the value of each product by a current average price index. The choice between the two approaches is important. According to Baumol and Wolff, the base year measure is a defensible index for productivity growth comparisons; however, it is not a useful indicator of inter-industry or inter-sectoral differences in absolute levels of productivity. Similarly, the deflated price index is meaningful for intra-industry comparisons of absolute levels of productivity over time, but it too fails to provide meaningful cross-section comparisons. The search for a valid cross-sectional index of absolute production must continue, according to these authors.

Second, the average product of labor is asymmetrically related to cyclical movements in business activity, and thus may suggest trends that are unrelated to technical progress. Gordon [121], for example, contends that firms retain more workers in the last stage of a business cycle than is justified by the future level of output. As a result of such biased expectations, Q/L will decline until firms adjust their hiring patterns to their (corrected) expectations about future demand.

Third—and perhaps most serious—labor (or capital) is not the sole source of productivity improvements. Labor-saving improvements resulting from other factors of production are improperly attributed as an improvement in labor productivity. Gold [117], among others, has shunned partial factor productivity indices precisely for this reason. A useful and meaningful productivity framework must, he contends, identify the sources of the productivity improvement and their interaction with other factors, such as capital and materials, in the overall production process. Along similar lines, Craig and Harris [68] show that partial factor productivity measures do not quantify the impact of technical substitition. If, for example, a new technology is embodied in capital, Q/L could rise as a result of capital for labor substitution, other things held constant. But if the cost of the new capital-embodied technology equals the cost saving from fewer workers, then total production costs are unchanged and the initial movement in Q/L is misleading with regard to "real" productivity gains.

4.2c. Total factor productivity indices

Solow's [318] pioneering study was the first to posit an aggregate production function explicitly. His "Divisia" or geometric index was formulated from a Cobb-Douglas production function written in terms of capital and labor, and was characterized by linear homogeneity and disembodied Hicks neutral technological change as

$$Q = A(t)K^{\alpha}L^{\beta}, \qquad (14)$$

where (assuming perfect competition), α and β ($\alpha + \beta = 1$) are the shares of income distributed to capital and labor respectively. From Eq. (14) it follows that the impact of technological change on production can be approximated by a residual growth rate. Taking the natural logrithm of both sides of Eq. (14) yields

$$\ln Q = \ln A(t) + \alpha \ln K + \beta \ln L. \tag{15}$$

Then taking the time derivative of both sides of Eq. (15), and rearranging terms, yields

$$\frac{\dot{\text{TFP}}}{\text{TFP}} = \frac{\dot{A}}{A} = \frac{\dot{Q}}{Q} - \alpha \frac{\dot{K}}{K} - \beta \frac{\dot{L}}{L}. \tag{16}$$

More descriptively, technological change, denoted by $\dot{A}/A$, represents the percentage change in output per year that is not explained by the annual percentage change in factor inputs. In other words, $\dot{A}/A$ is an "impact indicator." As Domar [86, p. 712] more realistically characterizes the situation: "A is a residual. It absorbs, like a sponge, all increases in output not accounted for by the growth of explicitly recognized inputs."

Diagramatically, the shift in production from period 0 to period 1 via A_0 to A_1 is shown by movement from point D to point A in Figure 3. $\dot{A}/A$ in Eq. (16) is approximated in terms of the line segment DE, while the change in capital intensity is approximated by the segment EA.

This Solow residual measure of total factor productivity growth has been used extensively in empirical research, especially in studies attempting to correlate technology investments with an $\dot{A}/A$. However, the index does not distinguish between pure technological change and changes in efficiency with which resources (properly measured), including technology, are used. This shortcoming has motivated the use of "frontier" production function studies [103].[18]

The Cobb-Douglas production function in Eq. (14) has several unique features. Technological change is simultaneously Hicks neutral, Harrod neutral and Solow neutral if the production function is Cobb-Douglas [347]. If $A(t) = e^{\lambda t}$ in Eq. (14), with λ being a parameter reflecting the rate of disembodied technological

---

[18] For one application, see Nishimizu and Page's [250] analysis of productivity change in Yugoslavia.

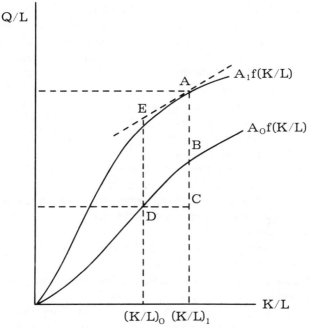

FIGURE 3 Discrete approximation of technological change as a shift in the production function.

change, then, following Stoneman [328], technological change is Hicks neutral at rate m:[19]

$$Q = e^{mt}K^{\alpha}L^{1-\alpha} = (Ke^{mt})^{\alpha}(Le^{mt})^{1-\alpha}, \qquad \lambda = m; \qquad (17)$$

and Harrod neutral at rate m:

$$Q = e^{m(1-\alpha)t}K^{\alpha}L^{1-\alpha} = K^{\alpha}(Le^{mt})^{1-\alpha}, \qquad \lambda = m(1-\alpha); \qquad (18)$$

and Solow neutral at rate m:

$$Q = e^{m\alpha t}K^{\alpha}L^{1-\alpha} = (Ke^{mt})^{\alpha}L^{1-\alpha}, \qquad \lambda = m\alpha. \qquad (19)$$

The explicit assumption of neutrality is a limitation associated with any total factor productivity index derived from a Cobb–Douglas specification [284]. There is some empirical evidence [e.g.,

---

[19] See Aukrust [11], Niitamo [249] and Valavanis-Vail [348] for early applications of such a production function form.

222, 290] that technical progress has been labor-saving over time (as originally hypothesized by Hicks [146]). Several specific empirical studies are worth noting. Moroney [232] found strong evidence for 1949 to 1962 that technological change was not Hicks neutral within U.S. manufacturing industries. In 11 of the 20 two-digit SIC industries studied, the bias was labor-saving. Cain and Patterson [44] reach a similar conclusion from an analysis of two-digit manufacturing industries over the period 1850 to 1919. Also using the Hicksian definition, Binswanger [28] and Binswanger and Ruttan [29] report that technological changes in U.S. agriculture (1912 to 1968) were biased. The changes were fertilizer-using and labor-saving, accompanied by a decrease and increase respectively in those factors' prices. Kopp and Smith [182] verified Binswanger's approach using four specific innovations from the iron- and steel-making industries.

The Cobb–Douglas specification also implies that the elasticity of substitution, σ, (a measure of the ease with which one input may be substituted for another at a constant level of output) is unity. This is thought by some to be a troublesome assumption because it fails to measure productivity gains which may result from changes that permit more flexible substitution of inputs in the production process. For example, consider a generalized two input production function that allows for non-neutral technical progress such as[20]

$$Q = F(K, L; t) = G(a(t)K, b(t)L). \tag{20}$$

From this more general specification, Hicks neutrality implies that $a(t) = b(t)$, that is, technological change is equally capital- and labor-augmenting. Harrod neutrality implies that $a(t) = 1$, meaning that technological change is labor-augmenting. Finally, Solow neutrality implies that $b(t) = 1$, meaning that technological change is capital-augmenting [278, 328].[21]

---

[20] A complete review of production function theory is not within the scope of this paper. Reference will be made to specific forms of production functions, but more complete reviews are in Walters [352], Solow [321], and Bridge [38], among other places.

[21] Gehrig [112] specifies other forms of neutrality: labor- and capital-combining and labor- and capital-additive. See also two important papers by Sato and Beckmann [293] and Beckmann and Sato [22]. Hayami and Ruttan [140] provide empirical estimates of factor augmenting technological advances.

The constant elasticity of substitution (CES) production function, originated by Arrow, Chenery, Minhas and Solow [10], is one case of such a purely factor-augmenting model:[22]

$$Q = [(a(t)K)^{-\rho} + (b(t)L)^{-\rho}]^{-1/\rho}, \tag{21}$$

where the elasticity of substitution is

$$\sigma = 1/(1 + \rho). \tag{22}$$

As in Eq. (7) above, the Hicksian bias B, may be stated [74] as

$$B = \left[\frac{\dot{a}(t)}{a(t)} - \frac{\dot{b}(t)}{b(t)}\right](1 - 1/\sigma). \tag{23}$$

Technical progress is, as suggested, not independent of σ. Technical progress is labor-saving as

$$\sigma \gtreqless 1 \quad \text{and} \quad (\dot{a}(t)/a(t)) \gtreqless (\dot{b}(t)/b(t)), \tag{24}$$

and the bias is capital-saving as

$$\sigma \gtreqless 1 \quad \text{and} \quad (\dot{b}(t)/b(t)) \gtreqless (\dot{a}(t)/a(t)). \tag{25}$$

Kalt [163] simultaneously estimated the rate of capital- and labor-augmenting technological change and the elasticity of substitution for the U.S. private domestic economy from 1929 to 1967. Using a CES specification, the elasticity of substitution was 0.76. The rate of capital-augmenting technological change was estimated to be near zero. Technological change in the U.S. over this period was labor-augmenting, implying, given the relationships in Eq. (24), Harrod neutrality.

Nelson [244] showed that there is little difference between results obtained when estimating productivity growth using the CES and Cobb–Douglas specifications. Rates of technical progress for the U.S. economy based on a CES specification are very similar to the Solow [318] Cobb–Douglas estimates [10, 22, 74, 100, 160, 173].

Kendrick's [164, 173] discrete arithmetic index of productivity change is consistent with a CES production function. The index is

$$\frac{\Delta A}{A} = \frac{Q_1/Q_0}{(wL_1 + rK_1)/(wL_0 + rK_0)} - 1 \tag{26}$$

---

[22] See Nerlove [248] for a review of works on the CES production function.

where w is the wage rate, r is the rate of return on capital, and the numerical subscripts refer to discrete time periods.

Constant returns to scale is an assumption frequently made when estimating the Cobb–Douglas and CES production functions.[23] This assumption, however, distorts the meaning of total factor productivity indices derived from Eq. (26) because no distinction can be made between pure Hicksian neutral technical progress and efficiencies resulting from an increasing realization of scale economies [326]. Sato [291] proves theoretically that such ambiguity can only be removed by estimating a non-holothetic production function for a given type of technical progress. (A production function is holothetic under a given type of technical progress if the scale effect and technology effect are indistinguishable.) From an empirical perspective, Walters' [351] reestimation using Solow's [318] aggregate data (1909 to 1949 for the U.S. economy) provides strong evidence that what was originally viewed by Solow as neutral technological change may have actually been growth due to production efficiencies resulting from economies of scale. Walters' estimates of annual technical progress are about one-third smaller than Solow's. Of course, Walters' estimates do not account for the interaction between technology and scale economies: as new technology embodied in capital enters production, the potential economies from an increase in scale also rise [305].

Finally, any total factor productivity indices that do not explicitly account for intermediate inputs, when constructing the denominator expression, or for the potential of factor substitution between intermediate inputs and capital or labor, are inherently biased. At the microeconomic level, the value of intermediate goods and services should be subtracted from gross output, leaving some measure of real value added to approximate Q. So doing implicitly assumes that the underlying production function is additively separable in the form $Q = f(VA + M)$, where VA represents value

---

[23] Constant returns to scale means that output changes in the same proportion as all inputs change. With reference to the Cobb–Douglas function in Eq. (14), this assumption implies that $(\alpha + \beta = 1)$. With reference to the CES function in Eq. (21), the exponent $(-1/\rho)$ implies constant returns to scale. The more general specification for variable returns to scale has $(-v/\rho)$ as the exponent, where v is the scale parameter [100].

added and M represents intermediate inputs [42, 84, 329].[24] If total factor productivity indices are to be reliable estimators, intermediate inputs must be accounted for on the input side [42, 86, 323].

Researchers have not only measured technical progress residually through a total factor productivity index, but they have also taken more explicit steps to account for the accuracy of input measures. Griliches [125], Denison [75], Griliches and Jorgenson [132], Jorgenson and Griliches [160], Gollop and Jorgenson [118], Christensen, Cummings and Jorgenson [53], Gollop and Roberts [119], Fraumeni and Jorgenson [104, 105] and others, have taken care to weight the components of labor and capital inputs properly to account more accurately for heterogeneous quality differences. Once done, as discussed below, the relative importance of real input growth for real output growth increases quantitatively.

The earlier theoretical works in this area (written in the 1950s) focused on the heterogeneity of capital. Realizing that new and more productive technologies can be embodied in successive vintages of capital, rather than simply augmenting (via $a(t)$) a homogeneous capital stock, Johansen [158] and Solow [319] conceptualized the following Cobb–Douglas vintage production function as

$$Q_v(t) = B(v)K_v(t)^{\alpha}L_v(t)^{1-\alpha}, \qquad (27)$$

where $Q_v(t)$ represents output produced at time t using capital of vintage v, $B(v)$ is a vintage-specific disembodied shift parameter, $K_v(t)$ is the stock of capital from vintage v in operation at period t, and $L_v(t)$ is the labor used with vintage v capital. Also at time t, the technology-adjusted capital stock $J(t)$ is

$$J(t) = \int_{-\infty}^{t} B(v)K_v(t)\, dv. \qquad (28)$$

There have been numerous empirical applications of the vintage model. The early studies were by Solow [319, 320], Nelson [243], Intriligator [155], Westfield [355], and Wickens [356], among others, using aggregate U.S. data. They failed to provide strong

---

[24] See also Terborgh [337] and Popkin [264] for suggested empirical resolutions of this problem.

support for vintage specifications. For example, Nelson [243] analyzed the U.S. economy from 1929 to 1960. He not only adjusted capital stock estimates for quality changes via Solow's $J(t)$ (as in Eq. (28)), but also adjusted the stock of labor in a similar fashion. Although $\dot{A}/A$ was generally a smaller number, "the embodiment effect . . . [was not] large enough so that changes in the rate of growth of capital fully explain the variations in the growth rate of potential GNP that the U.S. has experienced. . . ." [243, p. 590].[25] In addition, Nelson [243, p. 590] editorialized justifiably about the vintage approach:

> Somehow many economists have come to view the requirement that new technology be embodied in new capital as in some sense a happy phenomenon. The reason for this seems to lie in the greater sensitivity of the growth rate to the investment rate that embodiment implies. But surely, the less the requirements for new technology to be embodied in new capital, the less costly is faster growth. Of course it might be replied that if growth itself were an objective regardless of cost, and if it were easier to influence $\Delta K/K$ than other variables that affect growth, then a strong embodiment provides a strong handle for policy. But surely this is a strange argument.

Greater empirical support for the vintage models has come from cross-industry studies [123, 126, 136, 148], and from analyses focused specifically on the electric power industry [81, 111, 179]. Perhaps the most lasting contribution lies in more recent total factor productivity calculations [53] explicitly acknowledging the importance of capital quality adjustments (Eq. (27)).

Some recent productivity studies have continued to use Solow-like indices of technological change, but have incorporated several important new changes. First, careful effort has been exerted to adjust both capital and labor input measures for quality changes over time (and to adjust intermediate input measures accordingly in cross-industry studies). Second, alternative forms of the underlying production process have been estimated. For example, the studies

---

[25] A more detailed review of total factor productivity indices is by Domar [86]. There is not full agreement on the magnitude of the importance of the embodiment assumption. Nelson questions its empirical merits. Also, Intriligator offers some reasonable arguments as to why the vintage models are deficient at the macro level.

reviewed below have employed the transcendental logrithmic (translog) production function [55, 56], a production function introduced in order to capture more accurately the effect of scale economies and input substitution on a measure of technological change.

The framework for analysis is based on a three factor production function written in terms of capital (K), labor (L) and (t) as

$$Q = F(K, L; t). \tag{29}$$

Under the assumption of constant returns to scale, technological change is indexed as

$$v_t = \frac{\dot{Q}}{Q} - v_K \frac{\dot{K}}{K} - v_L \frac{\dot{L}}{L}, \tag{30}$$

where v_K and v_L are the distributive shares of capital and labor in the value of output. More specifically, when $F(K, L; t)$ is given the "translog" functional form:

$$\begin{aligned}
Q = \exp[&\alpha_0 + \alpha_L \ln L + \alpha_K \ln K + \alpha_t t \\
&+ \tfrac{1}{2}(\beta_{KK}(\ln K)^2) + \beta_{KL} \ln K \ln L \\
&+ \beta_{Kt}(t)\ln K + \tfrac{1}{2}(\beta_{LL}(\ln L)^2) \\
&+ \beta_{Lt}(t)\ln L + \tfrac{1}{2}(\beta_{tt} t^2)];
\end{aligned} \tag{31}$$

then,

$$\begin{aligned}
v_K &= \alpha_K + \beta_{KK} \ln K + \beta_{KL} \ln L + \beta_{Kt} t \\
v_L &= \alpha_L + \beta_{KL} \ln K + \beta_{LL} \ln L + \beta_{Lt} t \tag{32} \\
v_t &= \alpha_t + \beta_{Kt} \ln K + \beta_{Lt} \ln L + \beta_{tt} t.
\end{aligned}$$

Christensen, Cummings and Jorgenson [53] employed such a model for a comparison of growth patterns between the U.S., Canada, France, Germany, Italy, Japan, Korea, the Netherlands and the United Kingdom between 1960 and 1973 and for selected earlier periods.[26] At least two major conclusions came from their study: (1) cross-country variations in real product growth are associated with the growth of real factor inputs, and (2) any analysis that fails to incorporate quality changes in input measures will overstate the

---

[26] They also estimated relative productivity levels (1947–73) for the U.S., Canada, France, Germany, Italy, Japan, Korea, the Netherlands, and the United Kingdom. See also Jorgenson and Nishimizu [162].

contribution of total factor productivity growth to the growth of real
product.

The Gollop and Jorgenson [118] study focused on U.S. productivity growth by two-digit industry between 1947 and 1973. Accordingly, their production function explicitly included intermediate
inputs in order to capture, among other things, changes associated
with input substitutions. Gollop and Roberts [119] extended the
Gollop-Jorgenson model to account explicitly for domestically
produced and imported intermediate inputs within the production
function. They examined 1948 to 1973 data from the U.S. manufacturing sector. One important conclusion is that an indirect (as well
as direct) contribution by inputs to the rate of technological change
exists: "The indirect effect on technical change is a function of
substitution possibilities and the factor-using/factor-saving nature of
technical change" [119, p. 173]. In three-fourths of the manufacturing industries studied, the indirect effect of more costly imported
intermediate inputs (in particular, oil after 1973) was found to
retard the rate of technological change (and thus had an impact on
the slowdown in productivity growth during the mid-1970s).

Along similar conceptual lines, Fraumeni and Jorgenson [105]
determined that capital formation (real tangible assets) was the
most important source of the growth in aggregate value added
between 1948 and 1976. Also, the influence of reallocated capital
between sectors in the economy on changes in total factor productivity was found to be minimal. This conclusion differs in some
respects from the studies reviewed below emphasizing the effect of
inter-sectoral flows of knowledge on total factor productivity.

5. ALTERNATIVE FRAMEWORKS FOR MEASURING TECHNICAL PROGRESS/PRODUCTIVITY

5.1. Growth accounting

Any residually measured total factor productivity index confounds
the productivity gains achieved from better inputs and greater
organizational efficiency (movement toward the production function) with the output from process-related technological change (a

TABLE II
Growth accounting components of growth in real gross U.S.
product: 1948–66 and 1966–76 (in percentage points)

Components	1948–66	1966–76
Growth per Annum in:		
Real Gross Product	3.9	2.8
Tangible Factor Inputs	1.0	1.4
Total Factor Productivity	2.9	1.4
Advances in Knowledge	1.4	1.1
Changes in Labor Quality	0.6	0.5
Changes in Land Quality	0.0	−0.1
Resource Reallocations	0.3	0.1
Volume-Related Factors	0.6	−0.2
Government Activity	0.0	−0.1
Residual	0.0	0.1

Source: Kendrick and Grossman [172].

shift in the production function).[27] Beginning with Denison [75],
efforts were made to identify empirically factors underlying changes
in an index such as $A(t)$. In simplest terms, growth accounting is an
attempt to remove from the $A(t)$ residual all factors except a pure
technological change component.

Denison [75, 76, 77, 78, 79, 80], Kendrick [165, 166], Jorgenson
and Griliches [160] and Kendrick and Grossman [172] have pursued
this approach. For example, Kendrick and Grossman report, based
in large part on the work of Denison, that total factor productivity
growth can be decomposed into a number of categories. To
illustrate, consider the two recent time periods analyzed in Table II.
The average annual growth rate of total factor productivity in the
U.S. domestic economy between 1966 and 1976 was 1.4 percent
(second line). Advances in knowledge (for example, from R&D,
learning by doing and related experience) are estimated as accounting for 1.1 percentage points of this 1.4 percent increase; changes in

---

[27] Of course, what may be classified as organizational or management efficiency in
one firm (industry) may have resulted from a technological break-through or an
entrepreneurial insight in another firm (industry). This suggests the importance of
technology diffusion on the measured productivity growth of any one firm (industry).
This is not an issue at the aggregate level except in the case of international
technology transfers. It is an important issue at the microeconomic level.

labor quality (for example, changes in education, health, and the age/sex/skill composition of the work force) for 0.5 percentage points; changes in the quality of land for −0.1 percentage points; resource reallocations (such as inter-industry labor shifts) for 0.1 percentage points; volume-related factors for −0.2 percentage points (this included economies of scale, 0.3 percentage points, and intensity of demand, −0.5 percentage points); and government regulation for −0.1 percentage points. The residual (more accurately, the residual of the residual), or the "not elsewhere classified" component contributes 0.1 percentage points to the 1.4 percentage rate of growth. Jorgenson and Griliches [160] and Miller [226] were also able to explain fully the residual $A(t)$ by adjusting inputs for quality considerations and by more carefully accounting for aggregation biases.

Growth accounting studies illustrate the importance of measuring carefully inputs in the calculation of productivity indices. As well, such studies highlight the importance of technological change as an aggregate force driving productivity advancement. Partly in response to the findings from the early growth accounting studies, researchers began to focus on the micro-determinants of technological change, R&D activity in particular.

5.2. Output indicators

An alternative to total factor productivity measurement is to examine the direct output from the search for technical knowledge. This approach overcomes some shortcomings inherent in production function indicators of technical progress. Still the approach has problems [289].

One technology output indicator frequently examined is patent statistics [157, 240, 296, 304, 316].[28] Such indices of technological change are more directly linked to the invention stage. However, there are many well known problems with patent data. First, few results from scientific inquiry are patentable. Most patents come from R&D. In fact, Scherer [301] found evidence of a linear relationship between R&D spending and patenting activity in U.S.

---

[28] Sahal [285] refers to such measures as applications of the Pythagorean concept of technology.

manufacturing firms. Second, and more importantly, the propensity to patent depends upon corporate policy ("patent everything/patent nothing"), especially in high-technology industries where products have rapid lifecycles [216].

Alternatively, a chronology of major innovations over time has been used to quantify technological success [67, 210, 212, 213, 234, 282, 312]. One problem with such a measure is the definition of what constitutes a "major" innovation. For example, a seemingly minor innovation that diffuses throughout an industry may have a major impact on firms' productivity growth.[29] Studies by Baily and Chakrabarti [17], Mansfield [212] and Sviekauskas [331] have attempted to account for the relative importance of innovation.

A final output indicator frequently used is one that quantifies directly the impact of a technology on the affected system (a so-called systems concept [285, 286]). This approach is based on the belief that a production process is characterized not by a smooth production isoquant, but by limited input substitution possibilities. There are generic efficiency characteristics (e.g., motor horsepower, jet engine thrusts, computer operations per second) within any production operation (system). Therefore, attempts have been made to quantify changes in system characteristics and to treat such data as indices of the output of a new technology. Phillips' [262] study of aircraft technology examined system changes in DC-3 aircraft. Sahal [285] also followed this approach in his studies of innovation with regard to farm tractors and locomotives.

Output indicators may be relatively more useful for measuring technical progress at a micro rather than macro level, holding institutional characteristics constant.

5.3. Other approaches

Other imaginative and useful approaches to measuring technological progress employ either an input-output framework or a management decision framework.

Leontief-like [188] productivity measures are formulated from

---

[29] Relatedly, Link and Zmud [207] studied the innovative output of firms in the video display terminal industry by determining (from surveys) "the number of new products introduced [over a three year period] that were directly related to the use of an advanced technology not previously applied."

sectoral input-output models. These models begin with a linear functional relationship [85], as

$$x_{ij} = \alpha_{ij} X_i / A_i A_j, \tag{33}$$

where x_{ij} is the output of sector j consumed by sector i, the α's are the input coefficients, and X_i is the net output of sector i. Productivity gains are measured in terms of A_i and A_j. For example, if A_i increases, fewer inputs (that is, outputs from sector j consumed in sector i) are needed in sector i to produce a unit of output X_i. Carter [47] and Almon [9] applied this kind of model to portions of the U.S. economy, and Erdilek [92] and Moon [231] used it for case study analyses.

A number of other approaches to measuring productivity have been suggested [e.g., 12, 97, 115, 116, 117, 272]. Each is interested in measuring efficiency changes more precisely, but they do not focus as explicitly on the technology-to-productivity relationship as have the above-referenced writings.[30]

6. TRENDS IN PRODUCTIVITY GROWTH

6.1. International experiences

As we have seen, there are several approaches for measuring productivity growth rates. Partial factor productivity indices and total factor productivity indices are the most commonly used measures. Both have their merits and shortfalls.

Two measurement issues are important when comparing productivity growth. First, cross-country comparisons assume that the same production function characterizes industries in each country. This assumption is somewhat less troublesome when comparing productivity between developed countries than when making comparisons between developed and underdeveloped countries.[31] Second, indices should be standardized for differences in the value of output between countries. However, the common practice of using exchange rates to convert the net output from one country to the

---

[30] Eilon and Soesan [90] provide a useful review of the literature.
[31] Nelson [245] elaborated on the importance of this issue and proposed and illustrated an alternative framework.

TABLE III
Average annual productivity growth rates in nine OECD
countries: 1960–73 and 1973–79 (in percentages)

	Output/labor	Output/capital	Total factor productivity
United States			
1960–73	3.1	−0.1	1.9
1973–79	1.1	−0.2	0.6
Canada			
1960–73	4.2	1.1	2.9
1973–79	1.0	−1.6	−0.1
Japan			
1960–73	9.9	0.1	6.6
1973–79	3.8	−2.2	1.8
United Kingdom			
1960–73	3.8	−0.7	2.2
1973–79	1.9	−2.6	0.3
France			
1960–73	5.9	0.7	3.9
1973–79	4.2	−1.1	2.1
West Germany			
1960–73	5.8	−1.5	3.2
1973–79	4.3	−1.9	2.1
Italy			
1960–73	7.8	1.3	5.8
1973–79	1.6	−0.8	0.8
Sweden			
1960–73	5.8	0.1	3.6
1973–79	2.5	−3.3	0.3
Belgium			
1960–73	6.1	0.9	4.2
1973–79	4.4	−0.6	2.6

Source: Kendrick [171].

currency of the other produces inaccurate estimates because exchange rates proxy relative purchasing power poorly.[32] Therefore, cross-country comparisons so adjusted should be interpreted only as approximations of actual differences in productivity levels [183].

The data in Table III show decreases in the average rate of growth in labor, capital and total factor productivity between 1960–73 and 1973–79. Labor and total factor productivity growth between 1960–73 was greatest in Japan, although the rates for Italy

---

[32] Kravis [183] elaborated on this and related measurement issues.

are nearly as large. Growth rates in Japan were larger than those in the U.S. by more than a factor of three. Between 1973–79, the highest rates of labor and total factor productivity growth were not in Japan, but in Belgium, West Germany and France. In each of the nine countries, labor, capital and total factor productivity growth rates were lower in the 1973–79 period than in the 1960–73 period. Capital productivity decreased in every country between 1973–79.[33]

More detailed international data on total factor productivity growth are in Table IV. There appears to have been a decline in total factor productivity growth in all of the countries covered beginning around 1973.[34] As well, there appears to have been a decline in total factor productivity growth in the 1960s, compared to the 1950s, in West Germany, Italy and the U.S.[35]

In the Soviet Union total factor productivity growth declined from 1960 to 1975. The average annual growth rate from 1950–60 was 3.63 percent, 1.83 percent from 1960–70 and 0.26 percent from 1970–75 [23]. This declining trend has continued at least through the early 1980s [180, 354]. Using a rich set of enterprise data, Kontorovich [180] showed that waning technological progress contributed to the slowdown throughout the 1970s and into the early 1980s, as evidenced by a decrease in the number of technology-related activities (e.g., the number of new inventions).

---

[33] Other useful studies documenting the productivity slowdown in the European countries are by Boher and Petit [34] and Capdevielle and Alvarez [45]. Most of the empirical studies dealing with the slowdown in productivity across countries have tried to document the various rates of productivity growth, rather than to posit explanations for inter-country differences. There are exceptions. Scherer [304], for example, suggests that productivity growth remained relatively high in Japan in the 1960s because Japan started farther from the technological frontiers than other OECD countries after World War II. As the pool of technological possibilities in other countries was being replenished in the 1970s, Japan had positioned itself well to absorb this new knowledge, and thus was able to maintain its growth momentum. See also Giersch and Wolter [114], Peck and Goto [258] and Sato [292].

[34] Griliches and Mairesse [134] also substantiate this for the French manufacturing sector.

[35] Related works include Tinbergen [343], Domar et al. [87], Daly [72], Barger [19], Kuznets [186], Bernhardt [27], Evans [94], Hulten [153], National Research Council [241], Norsworthy [252], Nyers [255], Ostry and Rao [256], Prais [265], Yamada and Ruttan [360], Nadiri and Mohnen [238], and Giersch and Wolter [114]. An early review of some related literature is in Nadiri [236].

TABLE IV

Estimated average annual growth rates in total factor productivity: selected countries and authors (in percent)

	TFP growth[1]	TFP growth[2]
Canada		
1947–60	1.7	—
1960–73	1.8	—
1964–73	—	3.3
1974–77	—	1.1
France		
1950–60	2.9	—
1960–73	3.0	—
1964–73	—	5.5
1974–77	—	3.6
West Germany		
1950–60	4.7	—
1960–73	3.0	—
1964–73	—	4.2
1974–77	—	3.7
Italy		
1952–60	3.8	—
1960–73	3.1	—
1964–73	—	6.1
1974–77	—	2.0
Japan		
1952–60	3.4	—
1960–73	4.5	—
1964–73	—	9.5
1974–77	—	2.9
Netherlands		
1951–60	2.3	—
1960–73	2.6	—
United Kingdom		
1955–60	1.5	—
1960–73	2.1	—
United States		
1947–60	1.4	—
1960–73	1.3	—
1964–73	—	2.5
1974–77	—	0.7

Sources: [1]Christensen, Cummings and Jorgenson [53], [2]Nadiri and Mohnen [238].

6.2. The U.S. experience

Relatively more detailed data on productivity growth rates are available for the U.S. than for the other OECD countries listed in Table IV. Data for three broad sectors of the U.S. economy are presented in Table V. The productivity slowdown appears to have begun in the mid-1960s and to have accelerated after 1973. For example, the average annual growth rate of labor productivity between 1948–66 and 1966–76 fell from 3.5 percent to 1.9 percent, capital productivity from 1.5 percent to 0.3 percent, and total factor productivity from 2.9 percent to 1.4 percent. This declining trend also appeared in the manufacturing and farm sectors (with the exception of an increase in capital productivity in the farm sector between the two periods).

TABLE V

Average annual productivity growth rates: selected sectors in the U.S. economy (in percent)

Sectors	Output/labor			Output/capital			Total factor productivity		
	1948 –76	1948 –66	1966 –76	1948 –76	1948 –66	1966 –76	1948 –76	1948 –66	1966 –76
Private business sector	3.0	3.5	1.9	1.1	1.5	0.3	2.3	2.9	1.4
Manufacturing sector	2.7	2.9	2.2	0.3	1.0	−0.9	2.1	2.5	1.4
Farm sector	5.0	5.3	4.5	−0.2	−0.6	0.6	3.0	3.5	2.2

Sources: Kendrick and Grossman [172].

In the private business sector generally, and the sizeable manufacturing sector in particular, the post-1966 slowdown in total factor productivity growth was aggravated after 1973. Norsworthy, Harper and Kunze [254] report that the rate of growth in labor productivity in the private business sector fell from 3.3 percent between 1948 and 1965, to 2.3 percent between 1965 and 1973, to 1.2 percent between 1973 and 1978. Total factor productivity growth between 1973 and 1978 was lower than in any post-World

TABLE VI

Average annual total factor productivity growth rates in U.S. manufacturing industries (in percent)

Manufacturing industries	1948 -53	1953 -57	1957 -60	1960 -66	1966 -69	1969 -73	1973 -76
Food	3.3	2.5	1.1	4.0	1.1	2.8	3.7
Tobacco	1.1	3.5	4.8	2.0	3.6	3.0	1.1
Textiles	0.8	3.6	1.9	8.2	0.1	2.7	0.7
Apparel	2.8	1.4	1.9	2.0	0.8	5.5	2.5
Lumber	0.4	5.8	1.5	7.2	1.6	4.9	-4.7
Furniture	2.2	2.7	0.1	2.7	2.0	1.0	0.8
Paper	3.7	-0.4	1.7	2.8	2.7	5.3	-3.5
Printing, publishing	2.2	2.8	0.6	3.1	0.2	0.7	-1.0
Chemicals	1.8	4.3	2.5	5.0	2.9	4.7	-0.9
Petroleum	1.8	0.6	5.4	4.1	0.8	2.3	-1.7
Rubber	2.1	-2.4	5.7	3.6	3.2	1.4	-1.5
Leather	-2.0	0.7	3.0	3.1	-0.3	2.1	1.2
Stone, clay, glass	2.4	0.1	1.1	2.4	0.8	1.7	-0.9
Primary metals	3.2	-1.5	-4.1	3.3	-3.1	1.8	-3.9
Fabricated metals	1.4	0.3	2.0	2.6	1.5	0.9	-0.9
Machinery, ex. electrical	2.5	-1.9	1.1	2.6	-0.2	2.3	-0.5
Electrical machinery	4.4	2.0	2.6	6.2	2.9	3.7	1.6
Transportation equipment	3.2	1.5	3.3	4.2	-0.5	2.7	3.0
Instruments	4.6	0.6	3.0	3.5	3.1	-0.4	0.1
Miscellaneous	4.0	3.3	2.6	1.6	3.1	2.8	1.6

Sources: Kendrick and Grossman [172].

War II period, or in fact, in any period except The Great Depression, since the turn of the century.[36]

Average annual total factor productivity rates have been estimated by Grayson [122], Kendrick and Grossman [172], and Gollop and Jorgenson [118], among others, for two-digit U.S. manufacturing industries. As seen in Table VI, there is a significant amount of inter-industry variation in growth rates, both for any given time interval and between intervals. In general, the declining trend in manufacturing growth rates was led by primary product industries. Of course, one problem with analyzing such short periods of change is that they are not standardized business cycle phases.

---

[36] See the more detailed data reported in Kendrick [168, pp. 12, 15, 20].

7. THE PRODUCTIVITY SLOWDOWN: SOME CONTRIBUTING FACTORS

7.1. The issue at hand

Productivity growth is a fundamental contributor to overall economic well-being. Because of this, the persistent slowdown in productivity growth since the mid-1960s in certain countries, with a more pervasive slowdown since 1973, has caused considerable concern. Why has the growth in productivity been slowing? Has the structure of national economies changed so that traditionally measured indices are biased? Has the work ethic deteriorated in recent decades? Is it by chance that the productivity growth slowdown coincided with the world energy crisis in 1973–74? Has the pool of potential productivity-enhancing innovations dried-up? Or is it part of a longer-run cycle? Is the measured slowdown nothing more than a statistical artifact?

The last of these questions is very important. Has a slowdown actually occured? The data summarized in the previous section are highly aggregated, and, as such, are subject to error. One might ask: "Are we dealing with a sick patient or a sick stethoscope?" [145, p. 123]. Darby [73], among others, contends that the stethoscope is sick.[37] As noted earlier, a number of micro-level production studies have indicated clearly that the estimated residual $A(t)$ diminishes when input quality adjustments are made. But as Rees [271] observed, for such data problems to have been the sole contributor to the measured slowdown implies that downward-biasing quality mismeasurements must have been growing substantially during the 1970s. The opposite is more likely.

The researchers whose studies are summarized below have approached the productivity decline issue with varying objectives.[38]

---

[37] Darby [73] contends that there has been no substantial variation in labor productivity growth in the private economy since 1900 once adjustments for age, sex, education, and immigration are made to labor force data. As well, he argues that once quality adjustments are made, there is no evidence of a decline in total factor productivity growth either after 1965, or after 1973. Baily's [16] critique indicates that Darby's findings are sensitive to his methods of adjusting the labor force for educational changes. Alternative adjustments by Baily indicate clearly that the slowdown was real.

[38] This section draws from Link [202].

As a general rule, these studies attempt to explain the post-1965 or post-1973 movements in part by "correcting" partial or total factor productivity growth estimates for changes in efficiency-related factors that should be embodied in inputs, but which were relegated to the residual, or alternatively, by controlling for exogenous shocks that presumably altered the form of the underlying production function. That so many corrections have been attempted underscores the importance of fully understanding the simplifying assumption behind a productivity index before interpreting the index for what it is or is not.

7.2. Contributing factors: a menu of "independent variables"

Several factors related to the slowdown in productivity growth since the early 1970s are discussed below. Although most researchers agree that each of these factors is important, there is disagreement on the degree of their importance. This disagreement results in part from different econometric models and from differences in data measurement.

The discussion focuses heavily on the U.S. productivity slowdown. This emphasis reflects only the fact that substantially more empirical research has been published on the U.S. experience than on the experiences in other developed countries.

7.2a. Cyclical shocks

Nordhaus [251] suggests that the post-1973 slowdown in the U.S., while severe, is not unprecedented. His analysis of output per worker-hour in the nonfarm business economy between 1912 and 1979 led him to the conclusion that "while the [post-1973] slowdown may look quite unprecedented for those with short memories, in the longer view, the slowdown is one which we would expect to occur from time to time" [p. 153].[39]

Others agree that there are cyclical patterns in labor productivity estimates, but do not denigrate the importance of recent trends [15]. The fundamental issue hinges on whether the slowdown causes

---

[39] This conclusion is not inconsistent with Verdoorn's Law, which predicts a long-run relationship between growth rates of productivity and output [349].

are cyclical (due to changes in the composition of demand or the utilization of inputs, especially labor) or secular in nature (that is, long-run, due to inter-sectoral or demographic changes in labor or capital and technology-related investment behaviour).

Following Perry [260, 261], Gordon [121] and Mohr [230] contend that short-run cyclical movements in labor productivity are common. Gordon's empirical analysis confirms at least in part that a portion of the post-1965 slowdown in U.S. labor productivity growth was due to the "end-of-expansion" phenomenon brought about by cyclical labor hiring practices.[40]

Dickens' [83] empirical analysis of changes in U.S. aggregate labor productivity from 1954 to 1980 suggests that Gordon's end-of-expansion hypothesis be rejected in favor of hypotheses that there was a permanent productivity loss during the business cycle downturns that was not regained during the upturn of the corresponding cycles begun in 1966, 1973, and 1977. Allen and Link [8] contend that, as Gordon's analysis would imply, the cyclical component of the productivity slowdown dominates whatever secular trend may have existed in those three upturns. They find no permanent productivity growth losses. However, much of the remaining empirical research in this area is based on the implicit assumption that the U.S. productivity (labor and total factor) slowdown was due to secular changes brought about either by shocks to the economy or by imposed regulations.

Certainly, part of the slowdown in productivity growth experienced in the countries of Table IV, and in most countries throughout the world, was due to cyclical factors. According to Nadiri and Mohnen [238], about one-half of the slowdown in total factor productivity growth between 1964–73 and 1974–77 in the U.S., Japan, Canada, France, Germany and Italy was related to economic recession.

7.2b. Capital investments

Cyclical activity in an economy indirectly affects productivity growth by affecting capital investments. Changes in the growth of capital

---

[40] See also Kendrick [167] and Neftci [242].

are frequently cited as an independent causal factor explaining the productivity slowdown.

The framework for these analyses varies. For example, Maddison [209] compared the average annual growth rate of gross domestic production per man-hour to that of capital per employee in six countries between 1960–73 and 1973–80. Based on the data reported in Table VII, he concluded that a slowdown in capital formation was one factor explaining the productivity slowdown. Using a growth accounting framework, Kendrick [171] reached a similar conclusion for nine OECD countries between 1960–73 and 1973–79.

With respect to the U.S. economy, the size of capital's role in explaining the labor productivity growth slowdown changed after 1973. Prior to 1973, there is agreement that the slowdown was due less to a weakness in capital formation than to a decline in total factor productivity growth. For example, the growth rate of labor productivity decreased by 1.0 percentage point in the private

TABLE VII

Average annual growth rates of productivity-related variables: Selected countries; 1960–1981 (in percent)

	Gross domestic product per man-hour	Capital stock per employee	Adjusted capital stock per employee
France			
1960–73	5.5	4.8	—
1973–81	3.0	4.5	3.9
West Germany			
1960–73	5.4	6.2	—
1973–81	3.7	4.7	4.1
Japan			
1960–73	9.3	10.6	—
1973–81	3.1	5.8	5.2
Netherlands			
1960–73	5.4	5.9	—
1973–81	2.6	3.4	2.9
United Kingdom			
1960–73	3.9	4.2	—
1973–81	2.9	3.4	2.8
United States			
1960–73	2.6	2.1	—
1973–81	1.1	1.0	0.4

Sources: Maddison [209].

business sector between 1948–65 and 1965–73 (declining from an annual rate of growth of 3.3 percent to 2.3 percent). Between these periods Norsworthy, Harper and Kunze [254] calculate that 95 percent of the decline was due to changes in factors other than capital or labor. Denison [79, 80] and Fraumeni and Jorgenson [104, 105] reach a similar conclusion comparing the 1948–68 and 1968–76 periods.

The growth accounting frameworks used in these studies are based on an extension of the generalized production function in Eq. (29) and the definition of residually measured technological change in Eq. (30). Eq. (30) can be rewritten by subtracting the rate of growth of labor from both sides, and rearranging terms, as

$$\frac{\dot{Q}}{Q} - \frac{\dot{L}}{L} = v_K\left(\frac{\dot{K}}{K} - \frac{\dot{L}}{L}\right) + v_t. \qquad (34)$$

The left-hand side of Eq. (34) is the rate of growth in labor productivity. The first term on the right-hand side is the rate of growth in the capital-to-labor ratio, weighted by the distributive share of capital, and v_t is total factor productivity growth. The decline in labor productivity growth between 1948–65 and 1965–73 (or 1948–68 and 1968–76, depending on the study) was due primarily to a decline in total factor productivity growth, v_t. In fact, there is some evidence that the rate of growth in the capital-to-labor ratio increased between the two periods, especially in the manufacturing sector [13].

After 1973, there is evidence that the continued slowdown in labor productivity growth was due primarily to a decline in capital formation [58, 59, 170, 178, 181, 237, 253, 327, 336]. According to Norsworthy, Harper and Kunze [254], the decline in capital formation accounted for about 70 percent of the decline in labor productivity growth in the private business sector between 1965–73 and 1973–78.

There are several important issues regarding measurement of the capital stock. Capital is heterogeneous: it includes equipment, structures, land and inventories. One issue relates to the method of aggregating these components. Direct aggregation consists of adding the various asset components in constant dollars. Alternatively, a translog (or Divisia) index is based on adding the growth rates of the assets, weighted by their distributive shares. The difference between the growth rate in the translog index ($\dot{K}^T/K^T$) and the directly aggregated index ($\dot{K}/K$) is the growth rate of factors influencing the effective input of capital services, q_K, as

$$q_K = \frac{\dot{K}^T}{K^T} - \frac{\dot{K}}{K}. \tag{35}$$

A similar index also exists for labor, q_L. Accounting for quality changes that make effective capital (labor) differ from measured capital (labor) leads to a revised version of Eq. (34), as

$$\frac{\dot{Q}}{Q} - \frac{\dot{L}}{L} = v_K\left(\frac{\dot{K}}{K} - \frac{\dot{L}}{L}\right) + v_K q_K + v_L q_L + v_t. \tag{36}$$

In terms of the growth accounting studies noted above, and in particular Norsworthy, Harper and Kunze [254], quality changes in capital include changes in the composition of capital (i.e., changes in the asset mix among equipment, structures, land and inventories); intersectoral shifts in capital; and growth in pollution abatement capital. They estimate that these factors, along with the slowdown in growth of the capital-to-labor ratio, account for a significant part of the slowdown in labor productivity growth after 1973 . . . "[t]he 1973–78 slowdown is dominated by the effects of reduced capital formation" [254, p. 421].[41]

Baily [13, 14] also shows that capital is an important factor explaining the decine in labor productivity growth since 1973. He argues that the flow of capital services relative to the capital stock changed after 1973. Although the absolute size of the capital stock was relatively large during the 1970s, its economic value deteriorated due to obsolescence, perhaps resulting from the energy crisis, which rendered some capital economically inefficient. Along these same lines, Maddison [209] adjusted his cross-country capital estimates to incorporate the "Baily effect". His findings in Table

---

[41] One reason the capital-to-labor ratio declined was the relatively large increase in the U.S. work force between 1973 and 1981 (or later) owing to an increase in the female participation rate and the baby boom maturing. Whereas the U.S. experienced an increase in females and young adults into the work force after 1973, Japan experienced the opposite tendency. Maddison [209] suggests that this fact may explain part of the absolute productivity growth rate differential between the two countries.

VII show that labor productivity growth, i.e. gross domestic production per man-hour, declined after 1973 in the six countries examined, and that growth in the capital-to-labor ratio, adjusted by changes in the economic value of capital, grew slower after 1973 than the unadjusted ratio. This issue is discussed in more detail below.

A related measurement issue concerns depreciation of the capital stock. There is precedent in the literature for using both the gross capital stock and the net (of depreciation) capital stock when measuring real capital inputs. Analyses of data prior to 1973 are not sensitive to the choice of measurement; however, after 1973 the composition of capital changed away from structures to equipment. The latter asset has a much faster rate of depreciation, which suggests, if capital is not a one-hoss-shay, the net capital stock measures are more appropriate.[42]

7.2c. Inflation and energy prices

Clark [60, 61] documents a strong negative correlation between the inflation rate and labor productivity growth in the U.S. economy as far back as the early 1940s. While this relationship may be spurious, according to some, there are sound theoretical reasons for expecting inflationary tendencies to have a dampening impact on productivity growth.

First, during periods of unanticipated and/or prolonged inflation, there is less certainty about the "meaning" of price signals than during periods of stable prices. Because managerial decisions are made in an uncertain climate, there may be efficiency losses as planning horizons shorten [141, 156]. Moreover, forecasting and decision-making in the shortened time frame may be misguided. For example, as input prices rise during inflationary periods, it becomes increasingly difficult to determine what portion of the increase is general and inflation-induced, as opposed to reflecting changes in *relative* factor costs [60].

Second, managerial talent may be diverted toward short-run decision-making as a result of the increased factor price uncertainty

---

[42] Denison [80] uses a weighted average of gross and net capital. See also Wolff's [359] comments on Denison.

[60]. The ramifications may show up in an inability to estimate hurdle rates for investments correctly and in an altered attitude on the part of managers toward risk-taking [141].

Third, in addition to affecting the choice of an optimal input mix, inflationary tendencies can directly affect capital investments. Depreciation of plant and equipment is based on historical costs. As a result, prolonged periods of inflation will lead to a widened gap between historic costs and effective replacement costs. Thus, current profits and taxes on profits are "too high" *vis-a-vis* the level requisite for financing required investments [187].

One obvious phenomenon linked to the world-wide inflation in the 1970s was the energy crisis of 1973. Some writers contended that the 1973 crisis was the primary influence bringing about the post-1973 productivity slowdown. Siegel [314, p. 60], for example, states: "Energy prices stand as the single most important contributor to the 1973 [productivity] break."

It is suggested that the energy shock represented a structural change in production relationships. For example, Rashe and Tatom [267, 268] argue that energy is a substitute in production for capital and labor. Partial and total factor productivity growth thus declined in response to the energy price increases begining in 1973. Alternatively, Hudson and Jorgenson [151, 152], Jorgenson [159], and Norsworthy, Harper and Kunze [254] argue that capital and energy are complements in production. Increases in energy prices reduce the demand for capital and thus decrease investment. Total factor productivity growth consequently falls. Using alternative empirical methods, Coen and Hickman [64], Filer [102], and Siegel [314], found that increased energy prices significantly reduced measured productivity growth.

Comparing productivity growth rates in OECD countries between 1960–73 and 1973–79, Lindbeck [192] finds that "dramatic" *macro* disturbances between 1972 and 1974 are important for explaining the post-1973 slowdowns. He argues that one key disturbance was the OPEC oil crisis and the input reallocation adjustments which followed. Helliwell, Strum and Salou's [114] and Maddison's [209] analyses of OECD countries, and Sylos–Labini's [334] analysis of the U.S. and Italy, agree with this.

Baily [13, 14], Berndt [25], Clark [61] and Stein [324] question this energy shock hypothesis on the basis of their own empirical work and offer an alternative explanation. Berndt [26], for example, contends that input substitution in response to higher energy prices is a long-run phenomenon, and could not have accounted for the contemporaneous decline in productivity growth.[43] Also, Scherer [304] points out that there are very few actual examples of such substitution, and investments continued in energy-intensive sectors. What probably happened is that the energy shock greatly reduced the economic value of the capital stock. If true, then the rate of growth of the conventionally measured capital stock overstates the rate of growth of the effective capital stock, meaning that total factor productivity growth estimates after 1973 are probably biased downward. Baily's [13, 14] analysis of the role of capital formation in productivity growth is based on estimates of the effective capital stock, measured by adjusting capital by Tobin's q, a proxy for the market valuation of assets. Therein he concludes that the decline in effective capital formation after 1973 was a major cause of the post-1973 labor productivity growth slowdown.

7.2d. Government regulation

It has been suggested that government regulation (e.g., of environmental and work safety programs) reduces measured productivity growth because the compliance costs in the impacted industry are absorbed by diverting real resources (financial, technical and human) from activities that would otherwise increase output [2, 89, 233]. The adjective "measured" is important when speaking about the impact of regulation on productivity. There are benefits from regulation (such as improvements in the value and quality of life) that may not be captured fully in conventional indices. For example, if demand increases in industries providing the capital goods and services used by the regulated industry to meet regulated standards, then measured productivity in the supplying industry may increase if economies of scale are realized more fully. If this occurs, the induced productivity gains will be realized in the

---

[43] Bruno [43] contends, as do others, that the direct energy component of production is too small to account for the observed slowdown in productivity. His analysis for the U.S., United Kingdom, Germany and Japan supports the hypothesis that the rapid increase in the price of raw materials during the early 1970s was the culprit.

supplier's residual $A(t)$ index, rather than being traced as a direct consequence of regulation.

If firms in the affected industry comply with regulation by diverting funds from investment in newer vintages of plant and equipment, then the *effective* capital-to-labor ratio will fall, as will measured productivity growth. Also, if compliance reallocates funds from R&D expenditures, then productivity growth will fall. The linkage between R&D and productivity will be documented below. An alternative to the resources diversion hypothesis is that regulation simply renders certain production methods no longer economical [65]. No resource reallocation would then follow, but the capital-in-use to labor ratio will fall. On the other hand, regulation may induce investment in new, more productive techniques. When in use, these new techniques could increase productivity growth.

Several studies have investigated these propositions. At the aggregate level, Christainsen and Haveman [52] find that between 12 and 21 percent of the slowdown in labor productivity in U.S. manufacturing between 1958–65 and 1973–77 was due to government regulation *per se*.[44] Other industry-specific studies also find that regulation (especially in environmental, health and safety areas) resulted in lower labor and total factor productivity growth in the U.S. during the 1970s, compared with earlier periods [33, 69, 70, 120, 266, 299]. Denison [79, 80] and Kendrick [169, 171] estimated that environmental regulations in the U.S. contributed to about 10 percent of the productivity growth slowdown. Using the relative portion of gross domestic product spent on environmental regulation as an adjustment factor, Kendrick [171] estimated a greater regulatory impact in Japan than in the U.S., and the same or a smaller impact in other OECD countries than in the U.S.

Another test of the diversion of resources hypothesis was by Link [200]. He showed that the amount of R&D expenditures directed toward environmental compliance activities by firms in the U.S. chemicals, machinery and petroleum industries was negatively correlated with residually measured total factor productivity growth.

---

[44] Evans [94] and Scherer [298] support this view too.

7.2e. Unionization

One view of unionism predicts that unions will decrease labor productivity by reducing management's flexibility, introducing inefficient work rules, and limiting compensation based on individual production. In contrast to this view, some economists emphasize a "collective voice/institutional response" view (e.g., [108, 109, 110]). They argue that unionism (a form of collective organization) may increase the level of labor productivity (e.g., [40]). Unions are said to act as agents for workers by providing a collective bargaining voice. Productivity is enhanced through decreased turnover and the establishment of grievance procedures, work rules, seniority systems, and the like. In addition, unionization "shocks" management to reduce inefficiency.[45]

The influence of unions in the post-1965 slowdown is rather opaque. A number of studies have found that total factor productivity growth is negatively related to the *level* of unionism [172, 195, 200, 215, 332, 339, 340] and to changes in the level of unionism [150].[46] It is quite possible that a part of the post-1965 slowdown was due to the negative effects of past union power. Union coverage in the private sector has been declining since the mid-1950s, and it is doubtful that unionism will play an important limiting role in future productivity growth [149].

7.2f. Entrepreneurship

Although there have been many conceptualizations of who the entrepreneur is and what he does [143], one characteristic of entrepreneurship is an ability to create or deal with disequilibria. In an environment as dynamic as an economy is, constraints are constantly changing. According to Schultz [309, p. 443]:

> [D]isequilibria are inevitable in [a] dynamic economy. These disequilibria cannot be eliminated by law, by pubic policy, and surely not by rhetoric.

---

[45] Weisskopf *et al.* [353] contend that declines in the work effort of U.S. workers contributed significantly to the post-1973 decrease in labor productivity growth. To the extent that unions can act as a collective voice for labor, their presence could reverse this tendency.

[46] The literature on the impact of unions on the level of productivity, productivity growth and profits, is more vast than the studies cited here. See Hirsch and Addison [149] for a detailed review. See also Freeman and Medoff [109].

A modern dynamic economy would fall apart if not for the entrepreneurial actions of a wide array of human agents who reallocate their resources and thereby bring their part of the economy back into equilibrium.

This constant readjustment toward equilibrium stimulates productivity growth. According to Klein [176], the 1970s slowdown in U.S. productivity growth can be viewed in terms of a decline in businessmen's ability or desire to deal with disequilibria.[47]

Did the productivity slowdown stem from a lack of perception or ability by leaders to exercise entrepreneurial talents? The empirical evidence is wanting. Hayes and Abernathy [141, p. 70] suggest that the "rules of the game" may have changed in the U.S. What could be referred to as "managerial myopia" may simply be a rational response to either short-run profit incentives or to a market of managers that is in flux:

> [W]e believe that during the past two decades American managers have increasingly relied on principles which prize analytical detachment and methodological elegance over insight, based on experience, into the subtleties and complexities of strategic decisions. As a result, short-run financial returns have become the overriding criteria for many companies.

The importance of a changing entrepreneurial attitude is still in question.

7.3. A more focused look

To this point I have argued that total factor productivity indices represent an effort to quantify the impact of technical advances on production. Although conceptual and measurement problems remain, the post-1965 and post-1973 trends in total factor productivity growth for industrialized countries seem sufficiently robust to raise a question whether innovative activity slowed down. A prior question is: What kinds of activities spur innovation?

Although macroeconomic forces (i.e., those that shape investment in new technology) have influenced the productivity growth

---

[47] These disequilibria occur at levels of aggregation. Adjustments to dynamic change determine, in part, competitive strategies, the focus of R&D, and even worker motivation.

pattern, it is not enough to end the story simply with them. We must still attempt to explain the relationship between technological change and productivity growth in terms of the relevant linkages. One step toward that end is to examine at a microeconomic level the sources of technological change. A conceptual model of endogenous technical progress must indeed begin at that level.

8. SOURCES OF TECHNOLOGICAL CHANGE

8.1. A conceptual framework

Figure 4 outlines schematically the technological strategies and environmental constraints associated with the sources of a firm's technical knowledge.[48] As a starting point, it should be recognized that firms operate in a market environment influencing their innovative activities. Markets are traditionally characterized in economics on a continuum ranging from monopoly to pure competition. Although useful for discussions about price competition or competitive strategy, this characterization loses some applicability when technological competition is considered.[49]

A firm's technological environment can be described in several dimensions. The overall market structure in which the firm operates influences its innovation strategy, which in turn influences the methods used for acquiring/developing/modifying technology. For example, in mature markets where product competition is primarily in terms of price, a firm's technology response may emphasize process-related innovations aimed at reducing operating costs. In emerging markets, product development (improved quality or design) may be the appropriate strategy [207].[50]

A relevant strategy decision associated with an innovation stimulus is where to invest in new technology. The firm has two broad

---

[48] A preliminary version of this model is in Bozeman and Link [35].

[49] See Baldwin and Scott [18] for a review of the literature relating market structure and innovative activity.

[50] One representation of the environment that seems relevant is the Utterback and Abernathy [346] product-process life cycle model. Although some have criticized its formulation (e.g., [257]), it remains intuitively appealing and widely used [93, 142, 205, 276].

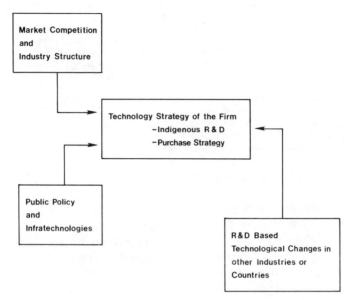

FIGURE 4   A conceptual model of a firm's technological strategy.

(but not mutually exclusive) choices: it can internalize the innovation process by pursuing specific activities, generally characterized under the rubric of R&D, or it can use existing markets to "purchase" the requisite generic technology.[51] This novel form of the "make or buy" decision is explicitly influenced by benefit-to-cost comparisons and implicitly influenced by the firm's R&D organizational structure and managerial philosophy [207].

The make or buy decision is illustrated in Figure 4 in terms of a dichotomy between R&D strategy versus purchase strategy. As the vintage production function models surveyed above suggest, firms can acquire new technologies by purchasing newer vintages of capital equipment. Other important sources include licensing and mergers. There is some preliminary evidence in Bozeman and Link [35] that manufacturing firms rely more on purchased technologies

---

[51] The issue of internalizing a market activity for which there exist alternative market mechanisms was first addressed by Coase [63] and later extended by Alchian and Demsetz [7] and Williamson [357, 358], among others.

TABLE VIII
Relative importance of alternative technology sources

Source	Mean ranking (Likert 1–5 Scale)
Indigenous R & D activity	1.3
Purchasing new capital equipment	2.7
Acquisition of firms through mergers	3.1
Licensing from domestic firms	3.7
Licensing from international firms	3.8
R & D conducted under government contract	4.2

Source: Bozeman and Link [35].

than on mergers or licensing as sources.[52] Listed in Table VIII are six alternative sources from which firms might acquire new technologies. Each technology source was ranked on a five-point Likert scale ranging from "very important" (equal to 1) to "not important at all" (equal to 5). Based on survey interviews with 146 R & D executives in technically active manufacturing firms, the relative importance of each source is denoted by the reported mean rankings.

R & D is not a homogeneous activity. It includes many categories of spending. The most common breakdown is among basic research, applied research, and development, but other categories are also meaningful: product versus process, long-term versus short-term, risky versus non-risky, offensive versus defensive, and so on.

R & D activity is one input into the innovation process. Innovations lead to technological change which, among other things, enhances productivity growth. Although it is common practice to associate R & D as synonomous with innovative activity, that practice is in error. As Mansfield [217] has shown in the chemicals, machinery and electronics industries, R & D costs do not account for the lion's share of expenses or time involved in innovation (the process going from research through manufacturing/marketing start-up).

---

[52] These suggestive findings were based on survey responses from R & D vice-presidents. They responded that indigenous R & D was the most useful source. The data also suggest that in industries tied to rapidly changing technologies, larger firms rely more on mergers (presumably with smaller firms) and smaller firms rely more on licensing (presumably with larger firms) as sources of technical information.

The idea of technological knowledge diffusing among firms has been explicit in the literature for a number of years. Early empirical efforts to quantify the extent of technology flows, other than through a more accurate measure of vintage capital, were made by Schmookler [307] and Terleckyj [338, 339]. More recently, Scherer [299, 303] and Link [201] have quantified the impact of R&D-related technology originating in industry i on measured productivity growth rates in industry j.

Even within an R&D unit, the knowledge brought to bear on research projects itself comes from numerous sources. Link and Zmud [206] identify twelve sources of technological knowledge frequently used by R&D groups in U.S. manufacturing firms. Table IX lists these sources, along with their frequency of use. R&D-performing manufacturing firms were asked to rank the sources along a 4-point Likert scale (always used equals 4, never used equals 1). The mean responses are shown. The most important sources are the firm's own marketing and manufacturing groups.[53]

The government also has a role in shaping a firm's technology-related activities. Regulatory activities influence R&D directly if meeting the regulation entails a substantial cost to the firm, or if it establishes product or process specifications that thwart or stimulate innovation. Also, the government frequently contracts with private firms for R&D-embodied products and finances basic research in industry and in universities. Federally financed R&D may complement or crowd out private R&D spending; and the arguments go both ways [147, 189, 190, 191, 196, 197, 218, 313, 333]. Third, tax policies are sometimes designed to encourage innovation. Fourth, and perhaps most overlooked, the government supports industrial infratechnology. This "infractechnology" includes the provision of public goods ranging from basic generic scientific knowledge to measurement standards and test methods [335]. By intention, the role of the government is to complement the innovation process

---

[53] The firm's choice of which sources to rely on for R&D intelligence is guided in large part by the nature of the firm's R&D spending. Firms doing basic research and reporting an overall imitative R&D strategy tend to use external sources more frequently. Internal marketing sources are more frequently used by firms whose R&D is primarily short-term in its focus. In addition, marketing and manufacturing may be ranked relatively high because of their knowledge of the firm's technological needs.

TABLE IX
Relative importance of sources of technological knowledge frequently used by R & D groups in U.S. manufacturing firms: 1981

Sources	Mean usage response (Likert 4–1 Scale)
Marketing group	3.15
Manufacturing group	3.12
Technical equipment suppliers	2.68
Customers	2.67
Professional interaction with peers outside of the firm	2.59
Informal interaction with peers outside of the firm	2.49
Universities	2.25
Consulting firms	2.09
National Technical Information Service	1.93
Other government agencies	1.90
Reverse engineering of competitors' products	1.92
New employees previously working for competitors	1.81

Source: Link and Zmud [206].

and, by diffusing technology-based knowledge, to increase the net social benefits from such activities.[54]

A firm-level perspective on innovation, as in Figure 4, emphasizes the role of diffusion in an endogenous model of technological change. The ultimate source of technology is knowledge; this knowledge comes from many places. Firms invest in themselves, so to speak, through R & D. But knowledge flowing into firms is perhaps equally important. Although some knowledge originates from unstructured creativity, much of the knowledge referred to in Figure 4 comes from R & D done in the private and public sectors. Therefore, at the aggregate level, there is some validity to models directly relating R & D to technology, but at a more microeconomic level, the relative importance of technology sources can only be understood with an appreciation of how knowledge diffuses.

---

[54] For early examples of the notion of technology diffusion, see Brown and Conrad [39], Evenson and Kislev [95], Massell [220, 221] and Schmookler [307].

9. THE TECHNOLOGY–PRODUCTIVITY RELATIONSHIP

9.1. A framework for analysis

Beginning in the early 1960s, researchers began to investigate quantitatively the impact of R&D spending on productivity. The framework used extends Solow's [318] model. A generalized version is outlined below [128]. The empirical applications are related to specific simplifcations in the following section.

The ith firm (industry, sector, economy, or whatever) is assumed to operate according to a three-factor production function as

$$Q_i = A_i F(K, L; T)_i, \tag{37}$$

where, as above, Q represents output, A is a neutral disembodied shift factor, K and L are measures of the stock of physical capital and labor (i.e., human capital), and T is the stock of technical capital available to the firm. T in turn can be written in terms of the alternative sources through which the firm acquires technical knowledge as

$$T_i = G(OT_i, BT_i, GT_i, IT). \tag{38}$$

Following Charles River Associates [49] and Tassey [335], OT_i is the ith firm's own (self-financed) stock of technical knowledge; BT_i is the ith firm's borrowed (or purchased) stock of technical knowledge; GT_i is the ith firm's government financed technical knowledge; and IT is the infratechnology affecting the firm. Most commonly, OT_i is assumed to be related to the firm's previous R&D efforts, RD, as

$$OT_i = \sum a_{i,j} RD_{i,t-j}, \tag{39}$$

where the accumulation weights a_j reflect the influence of a j-period distributed lag and obsolescence rate of R&D.

Early empirical studies employed a simplified version of this model, where the only argument defining T_i was OT_i and the production function was Cobb–Douglas:

$$Q = A e^{\lambda t} K^\alpha L^{(1-\alpha)} T^\beta, \tag{40}$$

where λ is a disembodied growth rate parameter and α and β are output elasticities. Constant returns to scale are assumed only with respect to capital K and labor L.

Using logrithmic transformations and differentiating Eq. (40) with respect to time t, one obtains the percentage change formulation

$$\dot{Q}/Q = \lambda + \alpha(\dot{K}/K) + (1 - \alpha)(\dot{L}/L) + \beta(\dot{T}/T), \qquad (41)$$

where again the dot notation refers to a time derivative. Residually measured total factor productivity growth is defined as

$$\dot{A}/A = \dot{Q}/Q - \alpha(\dot{K}/K) - (1 - \alpha)(\dot{L}/L) = \lambda + \beta(\dot{T}/T). \qquad (42)$$

The parameter β in Eq. (42) is the output elasticity of technical capital:

$$\beta = (\delta Q/\delta T)(T/Q). \qquad (43)$$

Substituting the right-hand portion of Eq. (43) into Eq. (42) and rearranging terms, we obtain

$$\dot{A}/A = \lambda + \rho(\dot{T}/Q), \qquad (44)$$

where $\rho = (\delta Q/\delta T)$ is the marginal product of technical capital and $\dot{T}$ is the decision unit's net private investment in the stock of technical capital.

In empirical work, if it is assumed that the stock of R&D-based technical capital does not depreciate, or depreciates very slowly, then $\dot{T}$ can be approximated by the flow of self-financed R&D expenditures in a given time period, RD, as

$$\dot{A}/A = \lambda + \rho(\text{RD}/Q) + \varepsilon. \qquad (45)$$

Estimates of ρ from Eq. (45) are interpreted as the rate of return to investments in R&D.[55]

Some of the more recent studies have assumed that Eq. (38) is additively separable in logrithms, and accordingly have included additional regressors in models like the one specified by Eq. (45). These other independent variables include the amount of federal R&D funds received, the amount of purchased or borrowed

---

[55] Scherer [299] demonstrates that if the R&D stock of technical capital depreciates at 100μ percent per year, then ρ would be biased downward.

technologies from other firms or sectors, infractechnologies, and disaggregated components of indigenous R & D.

9.2. A review of the empirical evidence

The literature on estimating equations like (45) can best be summarized by reviewing studies by the date of the data used, rather than by date of publication. Studies focusing on the early post-war decades reported a strong positive relationship between R & D and productivity growth. However, findings reported for later years are mixed. The studies have relied in general on U.S. data.

9.2a. The 1950s and 1960s

Minasian's [228] investigation focused on 85 industrial firms over the period 1947 to 1957. Using a simplified version of Eq. (45), he concluded that R & D was a significant determinant of productivity growth in chemical firms.

Griliches [127] reached a similar conclusion from his analysis of two-, three-, and four-digit manufacturing industries between 1958 and 1963. In [130], he extended the analysis to a 1957-65 sample of 883 R & D firms in six groups: chemicals and petroleum, metals and machinery, electric equipment, motor vehicles, aircraft and others. In total, and by industry, the R & D to productivity relationship was positive and even somewhat stronger in the more R & D intensive industries.

Perhaps the most extensive industry-level investigation of this time period was by Terleckyj [339] (based on [338]). He focused on 33 two- and three-digit industries between 1948 and 1966. Twenty of the 33 industries were in manufacturing. As with Minasian and Griliches, Terleckyj's estimated R & D coefficient, ρ from Eq. (45), was positive and significant. More importantly, Terleckyj extended Eq. (45) to include other R & D variables in an attempt to quantify inter-industry spillovers of R & D-based technology. First, a government financed R & D variable was added. However, its impact was zero (the importance of this result will be discussed below). Second, the impact of R & D embodied in purchased inputs (intermediate goods and capital goods) was also found to be significant. Given the magnitude of the spillover variables, he concluded that the private returns from R & D investment (estimated at around 30 percent) understate the full social benefits from R&D.[56] This work was extended in [299, 340, 341, 342].

9.2b. The early 1970s

In the U.S. economy, there was a modest decline in total factor productivity until about 1973 and then an accelerated decline from 1973 to the end of that decade. This post-1973 decline was intense within the manufacturing sector. Meanwhile, industrial R&D spending began declining in both relative and absolute terms during the late 1960s. Not surprisingly, researchers focused on the declining R&D spending pattern to identify a technology-based culprit for the 1970s productivity growth slump.

Total U.S. R&D as a percentage of GNP peaked at 3 percent by 1964 and then fell to 2.3 percent by 1975. There is disagreement regarding the quantitative impact of the R&D decline on measured productivity growth. On one hand, Nadiri [237] and Nadiri and Schankerman [239] estimated that the reduced rate of R&D stock accumulation may have accounted for as much as one-third of the post-1973 productivity decline. On the other hand, Denison [79] and Griliches [129] averred that the R&D slowdown accounted for at best one-tenth of the decline in productivity growth. Griliches posited that it was not the slowdown in R&D that was important, but rather, the "collapse" in the productivity of R&D itself.[57] Several empirical studies found that the R&D-to-productivity relationship documented during the 1950s and 1960s was no longer evident for data pertaining to the 1970s [4, 129, 194, 196]. However, Griliches subsequently changed his view on the basis of findings from newer micro data studies.[58]

9.2c. More recent works

Partly in response to the Agnew and Wise [4] findings and Griliches' [129] queries regarding the collapse in the productivity of R&D, a

---

[56] See also Griliches [124], Mansfield [211, 214] and Link [193] for estimates of rates of return using alternative frameworks.

[57] As Scherer [302] correctly notes, *if* Eq. (45) is specified correctly, one will always get a positive marginal return to R&D investments, even when the return function has shifted.

[58] Piekarz, Thomas and Jennings [263] suggest, based on a comparison of R&D spending patterns in 13 OECD countries (1963–81), that increases in the effectiveness (rather than the level) of R&D activity may stimulate both productivity and economic growth.

number of researchers began to investigate these issues. Griliches and Mairesse [135] examined a sample of 133 U.S. industrial companies for the period 1960–1977. The model was based on a Cobb–Douglas three-factor production function (which formed the basis for Eq. (45)). Cuneo and Mairesse [71] estimated a similar model for 182 French manufacturing firms between 1972 and 1977. Griliches and Mairesse [134] compared the productivity growth patterns between the U.S. and France *vis-a-vis* R&D spending patterns. In all three of these micro data studies, a strong relationship was found between R&D and productivity growth. This relationship was stronger cross-sectionally than over time. Griliches and Mairesse [134] were unable to explain 1973–78 differences in productivity growth rates between France and the U.S.

Clark and Griliches [57] also reported a strong R&D effect using data for 924 businesses (PIMS data set) between 1970 and 1980. They found no evidence that the return to R&D declined in the 1970s. Using the same data, Ravenscraft and Scherer [270] and Scherer [302] found a decline in the profitability of R&D during the early and mid-1970s, with a recovery in the late 1970s.[59] As to the reason why the profitability of R&D declined in the early and mid-1970s, Scherer [304] suggests that by the end of the 1960s the pool of technological opportunities had been "fished-out" faster than it could be replenished (with the notable exception of computers and microelectronic technologies).[60]

Mansfield [215] and Link [195] found a strong relationship using post-1973 micro data, after the heterogeneity of R&D is taken into account. Disaggregating indigenous R&D, they discovered a larger and statistically more significant regression coefficient on basic research spending than on applied research or development spending. Griliches [131] expanded the data set in his earlier analysis [130] and found similar results for the relationship between productivity growth and basic research spending.[61]

---

[59] See also Ravenscraft [269] for a similar analysis.

[60] Scherer goes on to explain that what perhaps happened was that diminishing returns to R&D set in, and by the late 1960s, real private R&D declined (until 1972) and then grew at a slower rate through the 1970s than it had before.

[61] On the basis of findings like these, Bozeman and Link [36, 37] proposed a tax credit for joint venture R&D as one policy alternative for increasing private expenditure on basic research.

Link [198] disaggregated R & D expenditure into activities aimed at process versus products improvements. The empirical results from a sample of 223 U.S. manufacturing firms for 1974–78 suggested that process R & D was more highly correlated with residually measured total factor productivity growth than product-related R & D. Scherer [299, 300] and Terleckyj [342] verified this finding.[62]

Scherer's disaggregated investigation [299, 303] exploited the Federal Trade Commission's Line of Business data on R & D. As with others, this disaggregated approach, with emphasis on carefully constructed productivity and R & D indices, substantiated that there still was (1973–78) a strong relationship between R & D and productivity growth. In addition, Scherer linked the R & D data with patent statistics to estimate inter-industry flows of technical knowledge. As expected, he found in general that process-related R & D impacted the "home" industry, whereas product-related R & D "flowed" to using industries.

The works of Scherer and Terleckyj have been extremely important in quantifying the importance of technology spilling over from one industry to another. This idea of indirectly borrowing or directly purchasing R & D-based technologies underlies the model shown in Figure 4. Link [201] estimated a model in which 302 U.S. manufacturing firms' expenditure on own technical knowledge and on purchased technical knowledge were included as regressors. Both R & D-related sources were shown to be important determinants of 1975–79 productivity growth. Relatedly, Suzuki [330] showed that R & D investments were significantly related to the rate of increase in labor productivity in Japanese manufacturing firms, 1965–1982. However, the rate of return to R & D fell after 1970 when Japan's dependence on imported basic technologies was declining.

Several studies treated federally-financed R & D as a separate

---

[62] Relatedly, Scherer [300] and Link and Lunn [203] found a relationship between seller concentration and productivity growth. Scherer found that labor productivity growth in 87 U.S. industry groups over the 1964–1978 period and 1973–1978 periods was greater in more concentrated industries. Link and Lunn contend that concentration affects the strength of the R & D—total factor productivity growth relationship. The returns to R & D, and process R & D in particular, were greater in more concentrated industries.

productivity determinant. Most researchers found a statistically insignificant coefficient for the variable.[63] There are two exceptions. Chase Econometrics [50] reported an impact from NASA-financed R&D on U.S. aggregate productivity. Also, Link [195] determined that federally-financed basic research was a significantly more important source than federally-financed applied research and development in enhancing productivity growth in a sample of 51 manufacturing firms doing federally-financed basic research over 1973–78.

The relationship of federally-financed R&D to productivity growth is not independent of its relationship with private R&D, and is perhaps not even direct. Beginning with Blank and Stigler [30], there has been a debate regarding complementarity ("pump-priming") vs. substitution effects between private and federal U.S. R&D. While much empirical evidence suggests a complementarity relationship, Lichtenberg [191] is skeptical. He contends that these results stem from an errors in variable problems.[64]

Link [199] argues that while federal R&D may complement the level of private R&D spending, it also lowers the productivity of that R&D. From an analysis of 51 U.S. manufacturing firms receiving federal R&D contracts between 1973 and 1978, he showed, using a model like Eq. (42), that the estimated return on private R&D is lower in those firms with relatively more contract obligations.

10. CONCLUSIONS

Many questions remain to be answered before we have a thorough understanding of the relationship between technological change and productivity growth and of the factors that influence both. That our knowledge on this topic is incomplete in no way denigrates the importance of the work reviewed here. On the contrary, the

---

[63] See Link and Ogura [204] for one theoretical explanation of the zero relationship between federally-financed R&D and residually measured productivity growth.

[64] Carmichael [46] is one of the few researchers to find a negative relationship between private and federal R&D.

number of scholars working on the problems is tribute to its importance.

Despite remaining gaps, several definite conclusions can be drawn:

1. Productivity growth is vital to the health of an economy.
2. The rate of productivity growth is influenced by the rate of technological change.
3. Technological change is influenced in part by the conscious efforts of the public and private sectors to foster innovative behaviour.
4. One importat investment in innovation is R&D.

One is drawn to speculate about the direction that research will take in the future. It is my belief that meaningful insights into the nature and consequences of technological change will be gleaned from richer investigations of behaviour at the firm level. Specifically, there is much to be gained from a more complete understanding of the sources of innovation within firms and the organizational factors influencing the efficiency with which these sources are realized and exploited. One should not be surprised to read a review essay on this same topic 10 years from now and encounter a bibliography stressing many more works in organizational theory and communications.

References

**[1] Abramovitz, M., "Resource and Output Trends in the United States since 1870," *American Economic Review*, 46 (1956), 5–23.

*[2] Abramovitz, M., "Welfare Quandries and Productivity Concerns," *American Economic Review*, 71 (1981), 1–17.

**[3] Afriat, S. N., "Efficiency Estimation of Production Functions," *International Economic Review*, 13 (1972), 568–598.

**[4] Agnew, C. E., and D. E. Wise, "The Impact of R&D on Productivity: A Preliminary Report," mimeo 1978.

**[5] Ahmad, A., "On the Theory of Induced Innovation," *Economic Journal*, 76 (1966), 344–357.

**[6] Aigner, D. and S. Chu, "On Estimating the Industry Production Function," *American Economic Review*, 58 (1968), 826–839.

**[7] Alchian, A. A., and H. Demsetz, "Production, Information Costs, and Economic Organization," *American Economic Review*, 62 (1972), 277–295.

**[8] Allen, S. D., and A. N. Link, "Declining Productivity Revisited: Secular Trends or Cyclical Losses?" *Economics Letters*, 15 (1984) 289–293.

**[9] Almon, C., Jr., *The American Economy to 1975: An Interindustry Forecast.* New York: Harper & Row, 1975.

[10] Arrow, K. J., M. Chenery, B. Minhas, and R. Solow, "Capital-Labor Substitution and Economic Efficiency," *Review of Economics and Statistics*, **43 (1961), 225–250.

[11] Aukrust, O., "Investment and Economic Growth," *Productivity Measurement Review*, **16 (1959), 35–53.

[12] Bahiri, S., and H. W. Martin, "Productivity Costing and Management," *Management International Review*, **10 (1970), 55–77.

*[13] Baily, M. N., "Productivity and the Services of Capital and Labor," *Brookings Papers on Economic Activity*, **1** (1981), 1–65.

[14] Baily, M. N., "The Productivity Growth Slowdown and Capital Accumulation," *American Economic Review*, **71 (1981), 326–331.

[15] Baily, M. N., "Will Productivity Growth Recover? Has It Done So Already?" *American Economic Review*, **74 (1984), 231–235.

**[16] Baily, M. N., "What Has Happened to Productivity Growth," mimeo, 1985.

*[17] Baily, M. N., and A. K. Chakrabarti, "Innovation and Productivity in U.S. Industry," *Brookings Papers on Economic Activity*, **2** (1985), 609–632.

*[18] Baldwin, W. L., and J. Scott, "Market Structure and Technological Innovation," in *The Economics of Technological Change*, ed. by F. M. Scherer. Harwood Academic Publishers GmbH, forthcoming.

[19] Barger, M., "Growth in Developed Nations," *Review of Economics and Statistics*, **51 (1969), 143–148.

**[20] Baudeau, N., *Premiere Introduction a la Philosophie E'conomique*, ed. by A. Doubois. Paris, 1910 [original in 1767].

*[21] Baumol, W. J., and E. N. Wolff, "On Interindustry Differences in Absolute Productivity," *Journal of Political Economy*, **92** (1984), 1017–1034.

[22] Beckmann, M. J., and R. Sato, "Aggregate Production Functions and Types of Technical Progress: A Statistical Analysis," *American Economic Review*, **59 (1969), 88–101.

**[23] Bergson, A., "Technological Progress," in *The Soviet Economy: Toward the Year 2000*, ed. by A. Bergson and H. S. Levine. London: Allen & Unwin, 1983.

**[24] Berndt, E. R., "Comments on Gollop and Jorgenson," in *New Developments in Productivity Measurement and Analysis*, ed. by J. W. Kendrick and B. N. Vaccara. Chicago: University of Chicago Press, 1980.

*[25] Berndt, E. R., "Energy Price Increases and the Productivity Slowdown in the United States," in *The Decline in Productivity Growth*. Boston: Federal Reserve Bank of Boston, 1980.

**[26] Berndt, E. R., "Comment on Jorgenson," in *International Comparisons of Productivity and Causes of the Slowdown*, ed. by J. W. Kendrick. Cambridge, Mass.: Ballinger, 1984.

[27] Bernhardt, I., "Sources of Productivity Differences Among Canadian Manufacturing Industries," *Review of Economics and Statistics*, **63 (1981), 503–512.

[28] Binswanger, H. P., "The Measurement of Technical Change Biases with Many Factors of Production," *American Economic Review*, **64 (1974), 964–976.

**[29] Binswanger, H. P., and V. W. Ruttan, *Induced Innovation: Technology, Institutions and Development*. Baltimore: Johns Hopkins University Press, 1978.

**[30] Blank, D. M., and G. J. Stigler, *The Demand and Supply of Scientific Personnel*. New York: National Bureau of Economic Research, 1957.

[31] Blaug, M., "A Survey of the Theory of Process-Innovations," *Economica*, **30 (1963), 13-32.

**[32] Blaug, M., *The Cambridge Revolution: Success or Failure?* London: Institute of Economic Affairs, 1975.

**[33] Boden, L. I., M. B. Zimmerman, and D. Spiegelman, "The Effects of Mine Safety and Health Administration (MSHA) Enforcement on the Cost of Underground Coal Mining." Final report to the U.S. Department of Labor/ASPER, 1981.

[34] Boyer, R., and P. Petit, "Employment and Productivity in the EEC," *Cambridge Journal of Economics*, **5 (1981), 47-58.

**[35] Bozeman, B., and A. N. Link, *Investments in Technology: Corporate Strategies and Public Policy Alternatives*. New York: Praeger, 1983.

[36] Bozeman, B., and A. N. Link, "Tax Incentives for R&D: A Critical Evaluation," *Research Policy*, **13 (1984), 21-32.

[37] Bozeman, B., and A. N. Link, "Federal Support of Industrial R&D: The Case of a Joint Venture Research Tax Credit," *Journal of Policy Analysis and Management*, **4 (1985), 370-382.

**[38] Bridge, J. L., *Applied Econometrics*. Amsterdam: North-Holland, 1971.

**[39] Brown, M., and A. Conrad, "The Infiuence of Research and Education on CES Production Relations," in *The Theory and Empirical Analysis of Production*, ed. by M. Brown. New York: National Bureau of Economic Research, 1967.

[40] Brown, C., and J. L. Medoff, "Trade Unions in the Production Process," *Journal of Political Economy*, **86 (1978), 355-378.

[41] Brozen, Y., "Determinants of the Direction of Technological Change," *American Economic Review*, **43 (1953), 288-302.

**[42] Bruno, M., "Duality, Intermediate Inputs and Value-Added," in *Production Economics: A Dual Approach to Theory and Application*, ed. by M. Fuss and D. McFadden. Amsterdam: North-Holland, 1978.

[43] Bruno, M., "Raw Materials, Profits, and the Productivity Slowdown," *Quarterly Journal of Economics*, **99 (1984), 1-29.

[44] Cain, L. P., and D. G. Patterson, "Factor Biases and Technical Change in Manufacturing: The American System, 1850-1919," *Journal of Economic History*, **41 (1981), 341-360.

[45] Capdevielle, P., and D. Alvarez, "International Comparisons of Trends in Productivity and Labor Costs," *Monthly Labor Review*, **104 (1981), 14-20.

[46] Carmichael, J., "The Effects of Mission-Oriented Public R&D Spending on Private Industry," *Journal of Finance*, **36 (1981), 617-627.

**[47] Carter, A. P., *Structural Change in the American Economy*. Cambridge, Mass.: Harvard University Press, 1970.

[48] Champernowne, D. G., "The Production Function and the Theory of Capital: A Comment," *Review of Economic Studies*, **21 (1953), 118-130.

**[49] Charles River Associates, *Productivity Impacts of Government R&D Labs: The National Bureau of Standards' Semiconductor Technology Program—A "Production Function Approach."* Washington, D.C.: National Bureau of Standards, 1981.

**[50] Chase Econometric Associates, Inc., "The Economic Impact of NASA R&D Spending," mimeo, 1975.

[51] Christainsen, G. B., and R. H. Haveman, "The Determinants of the Decline in Measured Productivity Growth: An Evaluation," in *Special Study on Economic Change*, vol. **10. Washington, D.C.: Congress of the United States, 1980.

*[52] Christainsen, G. B., and R. H. Haveman, "Public Regulations and the Slowdown in Productivity Growth," *American Economic Review*, **71** (1981), 320–325.

*[53] Christensen, L. R., D. Cummings, and D. W. Jorgenson, "Economic Growth, 1947–73: An International Comparison," in *New Developments in Productivity Measurement and Analysis*, ed. by J. W. Kendrick and B. N. Vaccara. Chicago: University of Chicago Press, 1980.

[54] Christensen, L. R., D. Cummings, and D. W. Jorgenson, "Relative Productivity Levels, 1947–1973: An International Comparison," *European Economic Review*, **16 (1981), 61–94.

[55] Christensen, L. R., D. W. Jorgenson, and L. J. Lau, "Conjugate Duality and the Transecendental Logrithmic Production Function," *Econometrica*, **39 (1971), 255–256.

[56] Christensen, L. R., D. W. Jorgenson, and L. J. Lau, "Transcendental Logrithmic Production Frontiers," *Review of Economics and Statistics*, **55 (1973), 28–45.

**[57] Clark, K. B., and Z. Griliches, "Productivity Growth and R&D at the Business Level: Results from the PIMS Data Base," in *R&D, Patents, and Productivity*, ed. by Z. Griliches. Chicago: University of Chicago Press, 1984.

[58] Clark, P. K., "Capital Formation and the Recent Productivity Slowdown," *Journal of Finance*, **33 (1978), 965–975.

*[59] Clark, P. K., "Issues in the Analysis of Capital Formation and Productivity Growth," *Brookings Papers on Economic Activity*, **2** (1979), 423–431.

**[60] Clark, P. K., "Inflation and Productivity Growth," paper presented at the Third Annual Conference on Current Issues in Productivity, Rutgers University, 1981.

*[61] Clark, P. K., "Inflation and Productivity Decline," *American Economic Review*, **72** (1982), 149–154.

*[62] Clark, P. K., "Productivity and Profits in the 1980s: Are They Really Improving?" *Brookings Papers on Economic Activity*, **1** (1984), 133–167.

**[63] Coase, R. H., "The Nature of the Firm," *Economica, New Series*, IV (1937), 386–405.

[64] Coen, R. M., and B. G. Hickman, "Investment and Growth in an Econometric Model of the United States," *American Economic Review*, **70 (1980), 214–219.

**[65] Collins, E. L., and E. C. Thomas, "The Tradeoff Between the Objectives of Environmental and Worker Health and Safety Regulations and Productivity," mimeo, 1978.

***[66] Committee for Economic Development, *Productivity Policy: Key to the Nation's Economic Future*. New York, 1983.

[67] Cooper, R. G., "Identifying Industrial New Product Success: Project NewProd," *Industrial Marketing Management*, **8 (1979), 124–135.

[68] Craig, C. E. and R. C. Harris, "Total Productivity Measurement at the Firm Level," *Sloan Management Review*, **14 (1973), 13–29.

**[69] Crandall, R. W., "Regulation and Productivity Growth," in *The Decline in Productivity Growth*. Boston: Federal Reserve Bank of Boston, 1980.

**[70] Crandall, R. W., "Pollution Controls and Productivity Growth in Basic Industries," in *Productivity Measurement in Regulated Industries*, ed. by T. G. Cowing and R. E. Stevenson. New York: Academic Press, 1981.

**[71] Cuneo, P., and J. Mairesse, "Productivity and R&D at the Firm Level in French Manufacturing," in *R&D, Patents, and Productivity*, ed. by Z. Griliches. Chicago: The University of Chicago Press, 1984.

**[72] Daly, D. J., "Remedies for Increasing Productivity Levels in Canada," in *Lagging Productivity Growth: Causes and Remedies*, ed. by S. Maital and N. M. Meltz. Cambridge, Mass.: Ballinger, 1980.

*[73] Darby, M. R., "The U.S. Productivity Slowdown: A Case of Statistical Myopia," *American Economic Review*, 74 (1984), 301–322.

**[74] David, P. A., and Th. van de Klundert, "Biased Efficiency Growth and Capital Labor Substitution in the U.S., 1899–1960," *American Economic Review*, 55 (1965), 357–394.

*[75] Denison, E. F., "United States Economic Growth," *Journal of Business*, (1962), 109–121.

*[76] Denison, E. F., *Why Growth Rates Differ: Postwar Experience in Nine Western Countries*. Washington, D.C.: Brookings Institution, 1967.

*[77] Denison, E. F., "Classification of Sources of Growth," *Review of Income and Wealth*, 18 (1972), 1–25.

*[78] Denison, E. F., *Accounting for U.S. Economic Growth, 1929–1969*. Washington, D.C.: Brookings Institution, 1974.

*[79] Denison, E. F., *Accounting for Slower Economic Growth: The United States in the 1970s*. Washington, D. C.: Brookings Institution, 1979.

*[80] Denison, E. F., "Accounting for Slower Economic Growth: An Update," in *International Comparisons of Productivity and Causes of the Slowdown*, ed. by J. W. Kendrick. Cambridge, Mass.: Ballinger, 1984.

**[81] Dhrymes, P. and M. Kurz, "Technology and Scale in Electricity Generation," *Econometrica*, 32 (1964), 287–315.

**[82] Diamond, P. A., "Disembodied Technical Change in a Two-Sector Model," *Review of Economic Studies*, 32 (1965), 161–168.

**[83] Dickens, W. T., "The Productivity Crisis: Secular of Cyclical?" *Economics Letters*, 9 (1982), 37–42.

**[84] Diewert, E. W., "Hicks' Aggregation Theorem and the Existence of a Real Value-Added Function," in *Production Economics: A Dual Approach to Theory and Application*, ed. by M. Fuss and D. McFadden. Amsterdam: North-Holland, 1978.

**[85] Dogramaci, A., "Perspectives on Productivity," in *Productivity Analysis: A Range of Perspectives*, ed. By A. Dogramaci. Boston: Martinus Nijhoff, 1981.

*[86] Domar, E. D., "On Measurement of Technological Change," *Economic Journal*, 71 (1961), 709–729.

**[87] Domar, E. D., S. M. Eddie, B. H. Herrick, P. M. Hohenberg, M. D. Intriligator, and I. Miyamoto, "Economic Growth and Productivity in the United States, Canada, United Kingdom, Germany, and Japan in the Post-war Period," *Review of Economics and Statistics*, 46 (1964), 33–40.

**[88] Drandakis, E., and E. Phelps, "A Model of Induced Invention, Growth and Distribution," *Economic Journal*, 76 (1966), 823–839.

*[89] Eads, G. C., "Regulation and Technical Change: Some Largely Unexplored Influences," *American Economic Review*, 70 (1980), 50–54.

**[90] Eilon, S. and J. Soesan, "Definitions and Prevailing Approaches," in *Applied Productivity Analysis for Industry*, ed. By S. Eilon *et al.* Oxford: Pergamon Press, 1976.

***[91] Elster, J., *Explaining Technical Change*. Cambridge: At The University Press, 1983.

**[92] Erdilek, A., "Productivity, Technological Change, and Input-Output Analysis," in *Research, Technological Change, and Economic Analysis*, ed. by B. Gold. Lexington, Mass.: D. C. Heath, 1977.

[93] Ettlie, J. E., "Evolution of the Productive Segment and Transportation Innovations," *Decision Sciences,* **10 (1979), 399–411.

**[94] Evans, M. K., "Productivity—Macroeconomic View," in *Special Study on Economic Change,* part 2. Washington, D.C.: Congress of the United States, 1978.

**[95] Evenson, R. E., and Y. Kislev, *Agricultural Research and Productivity.* New Haven: Yale University Press, 1975.

**[96] Fabricant, S., *Economic Progress and Economic Change.* New York: 34th Annual National Bureau of Economic Research Report, 1954.

[97] Farrell, M. J., "The Measurement of Production Efficiency," *Journal of the Royal Statistical Society,* Series A, **120 (1957), 253–290.

[98] Fei, J. C. H., and G. Ranis, "Innovational Intensity and Factor Bias in the Theory of Growth," *International Economic Review,* **6 (1965), 182–198.

[99] Fellner, W., "Two Propositions in the Theory of Induced Innovations," *Economic Journal,* **71 (1961), 305–308.

[100] Ferguson, C. E., "Substitution, Technical Progress, and Returns to Scale," *American Economic Review,* **55 (1965), 296–305.

**[101] Ferguson, C. E., *The Neoclassical Theory of Production and Distribution.* Cambridge: At The University Press, 1971.

**[102] Filer, R. K., "The Slowdown in Productivity Growth: A New Look at Its Nature and Causes," In *Lagging Productivity Growth: Causes and Remedies,* ed. by S. Maital and N. M. Meltz. Cambridge, Mass.: Ballinger, 1980.

[103] Forsund, F. R., C. A. K. Lovell, and P. Schmidt, "A Survey of Frontier Production Functions and Their Relationship to Efficiency Measurement," *Journal of Econometrics,* **13 (1980), 5–25.

*[104] Fraumeni, B. M., and D. W. Jorgenson, "The Role of Capital in U.S. Economic Growth, 1948–1976," in *Capital, Efficiency and Growth,* ed. by G. M. von Furstenberg. Cambridge, Mass.: Ballinger, 1980.

**[105] Fraumeni, B. M., and D. W. Jorgenson, "Capital Formation and U.S. Productivity Growth, 1948–1976," in *Productivity Analysis: A Range of Perspectives,* ed. by A. Dogramaci. Boston: Martinus Nijhoff, 1981.

**[106] Freeman, C., "Economics of Research and Development," in *Science, Technology and Society: A Cross-Disciplinary Perspective,* ed. by I. Speigal-Rosing and D. de Solla Price. Beverly Hills, Calif.: Sage, 1977.

**[107] Freeman, C., *The Economics of Industrial Innovation.* Cambridge, Mass.: MIT Press, 1982.

[108] Freeman, R. B., and J. L. Medoff, "The Two Faces of Unionism," *The Public Interest,* **57 (1979), 69–93.

**[109] Freeman, R. B., and J. L. Medoff, "The Impact of Collective Bargaining: Can the New Facts Be Explained by Monopoly Unionism?" mimeo, 1982.

*[110] Freeman, R. B., and J. L. Medoff, *What Do Unions Do?* New York: Basic Books, 1984.

**[111] Galatin, M., *Economies of Scale and Technological Changes in Thermal Power Generation.* Amsterdam: North-Holland, 1968.

**[112] Gehrig, W., "On Certain Concepts of Neutral Technical Progress: Definitions, Implications and Compatability," in *The Economics of Technological Progress,* ed. by T. Puu and S. Wibe. London: MacMillan, 1980.

**[113] Gelman Research Associates, Inc., "Indicators of International Trends in Technological Innovation." NSF final report, 1976.

**[114] Giersch, H., and F. Wolter, "Towards an Explanation of the Productivity

Slowdown: An Acceleration—Deceleration Hypothesis," *Economic Journal*, **93** (1983), 35–55.
**[115] Gold, B., *Foundations of Productivity Analysis*. Pittsburgh: University of Pittsburgh Press, 1955.
**[116] Gold, B., "A Framework for Productivity Analysis," in *Applied Productivity Analysis for Industry*, ed. by S. Eilson *et al.* Oxford: Pergamon Press, 1976.
**[117] Gold, B., "Improving Industrial Productivity and Technological Capabilities: Needs, Problems, and Suggested Policies," in *Productivity Analysis: A Range of Perspectives*, ed. by A. Dogramaci. Boston: Martinus Nijhoff, 1981.
*[118] Gollop, F. M., and D. W. Jorgenson, "U.S. Productivity Growth by Industry, 1947–73," in *New Developments in Productivity Measurement and Analysis*, ed. by J. W. Kendrick and B. N. Vaccara. Chicago: University of Chicago Press, 1980.
*[119] Gollop, F. M., and M. J. Roberts, "Imported Intermediate Input: Its Impact on Sectoral Productivity in U.S. Manufacturing," in *Aggregate and Industry-Level Productivity Analyses*, ed. by A. Dogramaci and N. E. Adam. Boston: Martinus Nijhoff, 1981.
**[120] Gollop, F. M., and M. J. Roberts, "Environmental Regulations and Productivity Growth: The Case of Fossil-Fueled Electric Power Generation," mimeo 1982.
*[121] Gordon, R. J., "The 'End-of-Expansion' Phenomenon in Short-Run Productivity Behaviour," *Brookings Papers on Economic Activity*, **2** (1979), 447–460.
[122] Grayson, C. J., Jr., "The U.S. Economy and Productivity: Where Do We Go From Here?" in *Special Study on Economic Change*, vol. **10. Washington, D.C.: Congress of the United States, 1980.
[123] Gregory, R. G., and D. W. James, "Do New Factories Embody Best Practice Technology?" *Economic Journal*, **83 (1973), 1133–1155.
*[124] Griliches, Z., "Hybrid Corn: An Exploration in the Economics of Technological Change," *Econometrica*, **25** (1957), 501–522.
[125] Griliches, Z., "Measuring Inputs in Agriculture: A Critical Survey," *Journal of Farm Economics*, **42 (1960), 1411–1427.
**[126] Griliches, Z., "Production Functions in Manufacturing: Some Preliminary Results," in *The Theory and Empirical Analysis of Production*, ed. by M. Brown. New York: National Bureau of Economic Research, 1967.
**[127] Griliches, Z., "Research Expenditures and Growth Accounting," in *Science and Technology in Economic Growth*, ed. by B. R. Williams. New York: John Wiley, 1973.
*[128] Griliches, Z., "Issues in Assessing the Contribution of Research and Development to Productivity Growth," *Bell Journal of Economics*, **10** (1979), 92–116.
*[129] Griliches, Z., "R&D and the Productivity Slowdown," *American Economic Review*, **70** (1980), 343–348.
*[130] Griliches, Z., "Returns to Research and Development Expenditures in the Private Sector," in *New Developments in Productivity measurement and Analysis*, ed. by J. W. Kendrick and B. N. Vaccara. Chicago: University of Chicago Press, 1980.
[131] Griliches, Z., "Productivity, R&D, and Basic Research at the Firm Level in the 1970s," *American Economic Review*, **76 (1986), 141–154.

*[132] Griliches, Z., and D. W. Jorgenson, "Sources of Measured Productivity Change: Capital Input," *American Economic Review*, **56** (1966), 50–61.
**[133] Griliches, Z., and F. Lichtenberg, "R&D and Productivity at the Industry Level: Is There Still a Relationship?", in *R&D, Patents, and Productivity*, ed. by Z. Griliches. Chicago: University of Chicago Press, 1984.
[134] Griliches, Z., and J. Mairesse, "Comparing Productivity Growth; An Exploration of French and U.S. Industrial Firm Data," *European Economic Review*, **21 (1983), 89–119.
**[135] Griliches, Z., and J. Mairesse, "Productivity and R&D at the Firm Level," in *R&D, Patents, and Productivity*, ed. by Z. Griliches. Chicago: University of Chicago Press, 1984.
**[136] Griliches, Z., and V. Ringstad, *Economies of Scale and the Form of the Production Function*. Amsterdam: North-Holland, 1971.
[137] Hahn, F. H., and R. C. O. Matthews, "The Theory of Economic Growth: A Survey," *Economic Journal*, **74 (1964), 779–902.
**[138] Harcourt, G. C., *Some Cambridge Controversies in the Theory of Capital*. Cambridge: The University Press, 1972.
**[139] Harrod, R. F., *Toward A Dynamic Economics*. London: MacMillan, 1948.
**[140] Hayami, Y. and V. Ruttan, *Agricultural Development: An International Perspective*. Baltimore: Johns Hopkins University Press, 1971.
*[141] Hayes, R. H., and W. J. Abernathy, "Managing Our Way to Economic Decline," *Harvard Business Review*, **58** (1980), 67–77.
[142] Hayes, R. H., and S. G. Wheelwright, "The Dynamics of Process-Product Life Cycles," *Harvard Business Review*, **57 (1979), 127–136.
*[143] Hébert, R. F. and A. N. Link, *The Entrepreneur: Mainstream Views and Radical Critiques*. New York: Praeger, 1982.
**[144] Helliwell, J., P. Sturm, and G. Salou, "International Comparison of the Sources of Productivity Slowdown 1973–1982," mimeo 1984.
[145] Henrici, S. B., "How Deadly is the Productivity Disease?" *Harvard Business Review*, **59 (1981), 123–129.
**[146] Hicks, J. R., *Theory of Wages*. London: MacMillan, 1932.
*[147] Higgins, R. S., and A. N. Link, "Federal Support of Technological Growth in Industry: Some Evidence of Crowding-Out," *IEEE Transactions on Engineering Management*, EM-28 (1981), 86–88.
**[148] Hildebrand, G. H., and T. Liu, *Manufacturing Production Functions in the United States*. Ithica, N.Y.: Cornell University Press, 1965.
**[149] Hirsch, B. T., and J. T. Addison, *The Economic Analysis of Unions: New Approaches and Evidence*. London: George Allen & Unwin, 1986.
*[150] Hirsch, B. T. and A. N. Link, "Unions, Productivity, and Productivity Growth," *Journal of Labor Research*, **5** (1984), 29–37.
*[151] Hudson, E. A., and D. W. Jorgenson, "Energy Policy and U.S. Economic Growth," *American Economic Review*, **68** (1978), 118–123.
[152] Hudson, E. A., and D. W. Jorgenson, "Energy Prices and the U.S. Economy, 1972–1976," *Natural Resources Journal*, **18 (1978), 887–897.
**[153] Hulten, C. R., "Why Do Growth Rates Vary?" *The Wharton Magazine*, (1981), 42–47.
**[154] Hulten, C. R., and M. Nishimizu, "The Importance of Productivity Change in the Economic Growth of Nine Industrialized Countries," in *Lagging Productivity Growth: Causes and Remedies*, ed. by S. Maital and N. M. Meltz. Cambridge, Mass.: Ballinger, 1980.
**[155] Intriligator, M., "Embodied Technical Change and Productivity in the

United States 1929–1958," *Review of Economics and Statistics,* **47** (1965), 65–70.

[156] Jarrett, J. P., and J. G. Selody, "The Productivity-Inflation Nexus in Canada," *Review of Economics and Statistics,* **64 (1982), 361–367.

[157] Johannisson, B., and C. Lindstrom, "Firm Size and Inventive Activity," *Swedish Journal of Economics,* **73 (1971), 427–442.

[158] Johansen, L., "Substitution versus Fixed Production Coefficients in the Theory of Economic Growth: A Synthesis," *Econometrica,* **27 (1959), 157–176.

*[159] Jorgenson, D. W., "The Role of Energy in Productivity Growth," in *International Comparisons of Productivity and Causes of the Slowdown,* ed. by J. W. Kendrick. Cambridge, Mass.: Ballinger, 1984.

*[160] Jorgenson, D. W., and Z. Griliches, "The Explanation of Productivity Change," *Review of Economics and Statistics,* **34** (1967), 249–284.

***[161] Jorgenson, D. W., and Z. Griliches, "Divisia Index Numbers and Productivity Measurement," *Review of Income and Wealth,* **18** (1971), 227–229.

[162] Jorgenson, D. W., and M. Nishimizu, "U.S. and Japanese Economic Growth, 1952–1974: An International Comparison," *Economic Journal,* **88 (1978), 707–726.

[163] Kalt, K. P., "Technological Change and Factor Substitution in the United States: 1929–1967," *International Economic Review,* **19 (1978), 761–775.

[164] Kendrick, J. W., "Productivity Trends: Capital and Labor," *Review of Economic and Statistics,* **38 (1956), 248–257.

*[165] Kendrick, J. W., *Productivity Trends in the United States.* Princeton: National Bureau of Economic Research, 1961.

*[166] Kendrick, J. W., *Postwar Productivity Trends in the United States, 1948–1969.* Princeton: National Bureau of Economic Research, 1973.

*[167] Kendrick, J. W., *Understanding Productivity: An Introduction to the Dynamics of Productivity Change.* Baltimore: Johns Hopkins University Press, 1977.

**[168] Kendrick, J. W., "Productivity Trends in the United States," in *Lagging Productivity Growth: Causes and Remedies,* ed. by S. Maital and N. M. Meltz. Cambridge, Mass.: Ballinger, 1980.

***[169] Kendrick, J. W., "Remedies for the Productivity Slowdown in the United States," in *Lagging Productivity Growth: Causes and Remedies,* ed. by S. Maital and N. M. Meltz. Cambridge, Mass.: Ballinger, 1980.

**[170] Kendrick, J. W., "Survey of the Factors Contributing to the Decline in U.S. Productivity Growth," in *The Decline in Productivity Growth.* Boston: Federal Reserve Bank of Boston, 1980.

**[171] Kendrick, J. W., "International Comparisons of Recent Productivity Trends," in *Essays in Contemporary Economic Problems: Demand, Productivity, and Population,* ed. by W. Fellner. Washington, D.C.: American Enterprise Institute, 1982.

*[172] Kendrick, J. W., and E. S. Grossman, *Productivity in the United States: Trends and Cycles.* Baltimore: Johns Hopkins University Press, 1980.

[173] Kendrick, J., and R. Sato, "Factor Prices, Productivity, and Economic Growth," *American Economic Review,* **53 (1963), 974–1003.

[174] Kennedy, C., "Induced Bias in Innovation and the Theory of Distribution," *Economic Journal,* **74 (1964), 541–547.

[175] Kennedy, C., and A. P. Thirlwall, "Surveys in Applied Economics: Technical Progress," *Economic Journal,* **82 (1972), 11–72.

**[176] Klein, B. H., "The Slowdown in Productivity Advances: A Dynamic

Explanation," in *Technological Innovation for a Dynamic Economy*, ed. by C. T. Hill and J. M. Utterback. New York: Pergamon Press, 1979.
[177] Klein, L. R., "Macroeconomics and the Theory of Rational Behaviour," *Econometrica*, **14 (1946), 93–108.
**[178] Klotz, B., R. Madoo, and R. Hansen, "A Study of High and Low 'Labor Productivity' Establishments in U.S. Manufacturing," in *Developments in Productivity Measurement and Analysis*, ed. by J. W. Kendrick and B. N. Vaccara. Chicago: University of Chicago Press, 1980.
[179] Komiya, R., "Technological Progress and the Production Function in the U.S. Steam Power Industry," *Review of Economics and Statistics*, **44 (1962), 156–166.
**[180] Kontorovich, V., "Technological Progress and Soviet Productivity Slowdown," mimeo, 1984.
**[181] Kopcke, R. W., "Capital Accumulation and Potential Growth," in *The Decline in Productivity Growth*. Boston: Federal Reserve Bank of Boston, 1980.
**[182] Kopp, R. J., and V. K. Smith, "The Measurement of Non-Neutral Technological Change," mimeo, 1983.
*[183] Kravis, I. B., "International Comparisons of Productivity," *Economic Journal*, **86** (1976), 1–44.
**[184] Kunze, K., "Evaluation of Work-Force Composition Adjustment," in *Measurement and Interpretation of Productivity*. Washington, D.C.: National Academy of Sciences, 1979.
**[185] Kuznets, S., "Inventive Activity: Problems of Definition and Measurement," in *The Rate and Direction of Inventive Activity*, ed. by R. R. Nelson. Princeton: National Bureau of Economic Research, 1962.
*[186] Kuznets, S., *Economic Growth of Nations*. Cambridge, Mass.: Harvard University Press, 1971.
[187] Lee, D. L., "Productivity, Inflation, and Economic Growth," in *Special Study on Economic Change*, vol. **10. Washington, D.C.: Congress of the United States, 1980.
**[188] Leontief, W. W., *Studies in the Structure of the American Economy*. New York: Oxford University Press, 1953.
*[189] Levin, R. C., and P. C. Reiss, "Tests of a Schumpeterian Model of R&D and Market Structure," in *R&D, Patents, and Productivity*, ed. by Z. Griliches. Chicago: University of Chicago Press, 1984.
*[190] Levy, D. M., and N. E. Terleckyj, "Effects of Government R&D on Private R&D Investment and Productivity: A Macroeconomic Analysis," *Bell Journal of Economics*, **14** (1983), 551–561.
[191] Lichtenberg, F. R., "The Relationship Between Federal Contract R&D and Company R&D," *American Economic Review*, **74 (1984), 73–78.
[192] Lindbeck, A., "The Recent Slowdown of Productivity Growth," *Economic Journal*, **93 (1983), 13–34.
[193] Link, A. N., "Rates of Induced Technology from Investments in Research and Development," *Southern Economic Journal*, **45 (1978), 370–379.
*[194] Link, A. N., "Firm Size and Efficient Entrepreneurial Activity," *Journal of Political Economy*, **88** (1980), 771–782.
[195] Link, A. N., "Basic Research and Productivity Increase in Manufacturing: Some Additional Evidence," *American Economic Review*, **71 (1981), 1111–1112.
*[196] Link, A. N., *Research and Development Activity in U.S. Manufacturing*. New York: Praeger, 1981.

*[197] Link, A. N., "An Analysis of the Composition of R&D Spending," *Southern Economic Journal*, **49** (1982), 342–349.

*[198] Link, A. N., "A Disaggregated Analysis of Industrial R&D: Product versus Process Innovation," in *The Transfer and Utilization of Technical Knowledge*, ed. by D. Sahal. Lexington, Mass.: D. C. Heath, 1982.

**[199] Link, A. N., "The Impact of Federal Research and Development Spending on Productivity," *IEEE Transactions on Engineering Management*, EM-29 (1982), 166–169.

*[200] Link, A. N., "Productivity Growth, Environmental Regulations and the Composition of R&D," *Bell Journal of Economics*, **13** (1982), 548–554.

*[201] Link, A. N., "Inter-Firm Technology Flows and Productivity Growth," *Economics Letters*, **11** (1983), 179–184.

**[202] Link, A. N., *Measurement and Analysis of Productivity Growth: A Synthesis of Thought*. Washington, D.C.: U.S. Department of Commerce, 1983.

[203] Link, A. N., and J. Lunn, "Concentration and the Returns to R&D." *Review of Industrial Organization*, **1 (1984), pp. 232–239.

**[204] Link, A. N., and S. Ogura, "A Note on the Complimentarity Between Public and Private R&D in the Production of Technology," mimeo, 1979.

*[205] Link, A. N., G. Tassey, and R. W. Zmud, "The Induce versus Purchase Decision: An Empirical Analysis of Industrial R&D," *Decision Sciences*, **14** (1983), 46–61.

**[206] Link, A. N., and R. W. Zmud, "Alternative Sources of Technological Intelligence: An Empirical Assessment of Managerial Strategies," mimeo, 1984.

[207] Link, A. N., and R. W. Zmud, "R&D Patterns in the Video Display Terminal Industry," *Journal of Product Innovation Management*, **2 (1984), 106–115.

**[208] Machlup, F., *Knowledge and Knowledge Production*. Princeton: Princeton University Press, 1980.

*[209] Maddison, A., "Comparative Analysis of the Productivity Situation in the Advanced Capitalist Countries," in *International Comparisons of Productivity and Causes of the Slowdown*, ed. by J. W. Kendrick. Cambridge, Mass.: Ballinger, 1984.

**[210] Maidique, M. A., and B. J. Zirger, "A Study of Success and Failure in Product Innovation: The Case of the U.S. Electronics Industry," *IEEE Transactions on Engineering Management*, EM-31 (1984), 192–203.

[211] Mansfield, E., "Rates of Return from Industrial Research and Development," *American Economic Review*, **55 (1965), 310–322.

**[212] Mansfield, E., *Industrial Research and Technological Innovation: An Econometric Analysis*. New York: W. W. Norton, 1968.

**[213] Mansfield, E., *Technological Change*. New York: W. W. Norton, 1971.

*[214] Mansfield, E., "Social and Private Rates of Return from Industrial Innovations," *Quarterly Journal of Economics*, **91** (1977), 221–240.

*[215] Mansfield, E., "Basic Research and Productivity Increase in Manufacturing," *American Economic Review*, **70** (1980), 863–873.

*[216] Mansfield, E., "Patents and Innovation: An Empirical Study," *Management Science*, forthcoming.

**[217] Mansfield, E., J. Rapoport, J. Schnee, S. Wagner, and M. Hamburger, *Research and Innovation in the Modern Corporation*. New York: W. W. Norton, 1971.

*[218] Mansfield, E., and L. Switzer, "The Effects of Federal Support on

Company-Financed R&D: The Case of Energy," *Management Science*, **30** (1984), 562–571.
***[219] Mark, J. A., "Productivity Trends and Prospects," in *Special Study on Economic Change*, part 2. Washington, D.C.: Congress of the United States, 1978.
[220] Massell, B. F., "Capital Formation and Technical Change in U.S. Manufacturing," *Review of Economics and Statistics*, **42 (1960), 182–188.
[221] Massell, B. F., "Aggregate and Multiplicative Production Functions," *Economic Journal*, **74 (1964), 224–228.
[222] May, J., and M. Denny, "Factor Augmenting Technical Progress in U.S. Manufacturing," *International Economic Review*, **20 (1979), 759–774.
[223] McCain, R. A., "Induced Bias in Technical Innovations Including Product Innovation in a Model of Economic Growth," *Economic Journal*, **84 (1974), 959–966.
[224] McIntire, J. L., "Problems with the Measurement of Productivity," in *Special Study of Economic Change*, vol. **10. Washington, D.C.: Congress of the United States, 1980.
***[225] Merton, R., "Fluctuations in the Rate of Industrial Invention," *Quarterly Journal of Economics*, **49** (1935), 454–474.
[226] Miller, E. M., "Capital Aggregation in the Presence of Obsolescence-Inducing Technical Change," *Review of Income and Wealth*, **29 (1983), 283–296.
**[227] Mills, F. C., *Productivity and Economic Progress*. National Bureau of Economic Research Occasional Paper 38, 1952.
**[228] Minasian, J. R., "The Economics of Research and Development," in *The Rate and Direction of Inventive Activity: Economic and Social Factors*, ed. by R. R. Nelson. New York: National Bureau of Economic Research, 1962.
[229] Mohr, L. B., "Determinants of Innovations in Organizations," *American Political Science Review*, **63 (1969), 111–126.
*[230] Mohr, M. F., "The Long-Term Structure of Production, Factor Demand, and Factor Productivity in U.S. Manufacturing Industries," in *New Developments in Productivity Measurement and Analysis*, ed. by J. W. Kendrick and B. N. Vaccara. Chicago: University of Chicago Press, 1980.
**[231] Moon, D., "Technological Change and Productivity in Input-Output Analysis and the Potential of Sectoral Optimization Models," in *Aggregate and Industry-Level Productivity Analyses*, ed. by A. Dogramaci and N. R. Adam. Boston: Martinus Nijhoff, 1981.
**[232] Moroney, J., *The Structure of Production in American Manufacturing*. Chapel Hill: University of North Carolina Press, 1972.
**[233] Myers, J. G., and L. Nakamura, "Data Adequacy for Productivity Analysis: A Case Study of the Primary Paper Industry," in *Measurement and Interpretation of Productivity*. Washington, D.C.: National Academy of Sciences, 1979.
**[234] Myers, S., and D. G. Marquis, *Successful Industrial Innovations*. Washington, D.C.: National Science Foundation Report NSF 69–17, 1969.
[235] Nadiri, M. I., "Some Approaches to the Theory and Measurement of Total Factor Productivity: A Survey," *Journal of Economic Literature*, **8 (1970), 1137–1177.
[236] Nadiri, M. I., "International Studies of Factor Inputs and Total Factor Productivity: A Brief Survey," *Review of Income and Wealth*, **18 (1972), 129–154.

[237] Nadiri, M. I., "Sectoral Productivity Slowdown," *American Economic Review*, **70 (1980), 349–352.

**[238] Nadiri, M. I., and P. Mohnen, "Sources of the Productivity Slowdown: An International Comparison," mimeo, 1981.

[239] Nadiri, M. I., and M. A. Schankerman, "Technical Change, Returns to Scale, and the Productivity Slowdown," *American Economic Review*, **71 (1981), 314–319.

**[240] Narin, F., M. P. Carpenter, and P. Woolf, "Technological Performance Assessments Based on Patents and Patent Citations," *IEEE Transactions on Engineering Managment*, EM-31 (1984), 172–183.

**[241] National Research Council, *Measurement and Interpretation of Productivity*. Washington, D.C.: National Academy of Sciences, 1979.

**[242] Neftci, S. N., "The Asymmetric Behavior of Labor Productivity During the Business Cycle," in *Aggregate and Industry-Level Productivity Analysis*, ed. by A. Dogramaci and N. R. Adam. Boston: Martinus Nijhoff, 1981.

*[243] Nelson, R. R., "Aggregate Production Functions and Medium-Range Growth Projections," *American Economic Review*, **54** (1964), 575–606.

[244] Nelson, R. R., "The CES Production Function and Economic Growth Projections," *Review of Economics and Statistics*, **47 (1965), 326–328.

[245] Nelson, R. R., "A Diffusion Model of International Productivity Differences in Manufacturing Industry," *American Economic Review*, **43 (1968), 1219–1248.

*[246] Nelson, R. R., "Research on Productivity Growth and Productivity Differences: Dead Ends and New Departures," *Journal of Economic Literature*, **19** (1981), 1029–1064.

**[247] Nelson, R. R., and S. G. Winter, *An Evolutionary Theory of Economic Change*. Cambridge, Mass.: Harvard University Press, 1982.

**[248] Nerlove, M., "Recent Empirical Studies of the CES and Related Production Functions," in *The Theory and Empirical Analysis of Production*, ed. by M. Brown. New York: Columbia University Press, 1967.

[249] Niitamo, O., "Development of Productivity in Finnish Industry," *Productivity Measurement Review*, **15 (1958), 30–41.

[250] Nishimizu, M., and J. M. Page, Jr., "Total Factor Productivity Growth, Technological Progress and Technical Efficiency Change: Dimensions of Productivity Change in Yugoslavia, 1965–78," *Economic Journal*, **92 (1982), 920–936.

***[251] Nordhaus, W. D., "Policy Responses to the Productivity Slowdown," in *The Decline in Productivity Growth*. Boston: Federal Reserve Bank of Boston, 1980.

**[252] Norsworthy, J. R., "Recent Productivity Trends in the U.S. and Japan." Paper presented before the U.S. Senate Subcommittee on Employment and Productivity, 1982.

*[253] Norsworthy, J. R., and M. J. Harper, "The Role of Capital Formation in the Recent Slowdown in Productivity Growth," in *Aggregate and Industry-Level Productivity Analyses*, ed. by A. Dogramaci and N. R. Adam. Boston: Martinus Nijhoff, 1981.

*[254] Norsworthy, J. R., M. J. Harper, and K. Kunze, "The Slowdown in Productivity Growth: An Analysis of Some Contributing Factors," *Brookings Papers on Economic Activity*, (1979), 387–421.

[255] Nyers, J., "Comparisons of the Productivity Levels of Austrian and Hungarian Industry: Methods and Results," *Review of Income and Wealth*, **28 (1982), 431–447.

**[256] Ostry, S., and P. S. Rao, "Productivity Trends in Canada," in *Lagging Productivity Growth; Causes and Remedies*, ed. by S. Maital and N. M. Meltz. Cambridge, Mass.: Ballinger, 1980.

**[257] Pavitt, K., and R. Rothwell, "A Comment on 'A Dynamic Model of Process and Product Innovation'," *Omega, The International Journal of Management Science*, 4 (1976), 375–377.

**[258] Peck, J., and A. Goto, "Technology and Economic Growth," *Research Policy*, 10 (1981), 222–243.

**[259] Perloff, J. M., and M. L. Wachter, "The Productivity Slowdown: A Labor Problem?" in *The Decline in Productivity Growth*. Boston: Federal Reserve Bank of Boston, 1980.

*[260] Perry, G. L., "Labor Force Structure, Potential Output, and Productivity," *Brookings Papers on Economic Activity*, 3 (1971), 533–565.

*[261] Perry, G. L., "Potential Output and Productivity," *Brookings Papers on Economic Activity*, 1 (1977), 11–47.

**[262] Phillips, A., "Air Transportation in the U.S.," in *Technological Change in Regulated Industries*, ed. by W. M. Capron. Washington, D.C.: Brookings Institution, 1971.

**[263] Piekarz, R., E. Thomas, and D. Jennings, "International Comparisons of Research and Development Expenditures," in *International Comparisons of Productivity and Causes of the Slowdown*, ed. by J. W. Kendrick. Cambridge, Mass.: Ballinger, 1984.

**[264] Popkin, J., "Comparison of Industry Output Measures in Manufacturing," in *Measurement and Interpretation of Productivity*, Washington, D.C.: National Academy of Sciences, 1979.

**[265] Prais, S. J., *Productivity and Industrial Structure*. Cambridge: At The University Press, 1981.

**[266] Priest, W. C., "Methodology for a Microeconomic Case Study of Productivity and Regulation: The Asbestos Industry," mimeo, 1981.

**[267] Rasche, R. M., and J. A. Tatom, "The Effects of the New Energy Regime on Economic Capacity, Production, and Prices," *Federal Reserve Bank of St. Louis Review*, 59 (1977), 2–12.

**[268] Rasche, R. M., and J. A. Tatom, "Energy Resources and Potential GNP," *Federal Reserve Bank of St. Louis Review*, 59 (1977), 10–21.

**[269] Ravenscraft, D., "Structure-Profit Relationship at the Line of Business and Industry Level," *Review of Economics and Statistics*, 65 (1983), 22–31.

*[270] Ravenscraft, D., and F. M. Scherer, "The Lag Structure of Returns to R&D," *Applied Economics*, 14 (1982), 603–620.

**[271] Rees, A., "On Interpreting Productivity Change," in *Lagging Productivity Growth: Causes and Remedies*, ed. by S. Maital and N. M. Meltz. Cambridge, Mass.: Ballinger, 1980.

**[272] Risk, J. M. S., "Productivity Yardsticks," *Management Accounting*, 43 (1965), 381–391.

**[273] Robinson, J., "The Classification of Inventions," *Review of Economic Studies*, 5 (1938), 139–142.

**[274] Robinson, J., "The Production Function and the Theory of Capital," *Review of Economic Studies*, 21 (1953), 81–106.

**[275] Robinson, J., "The Production Function," *Economic Journal*, 65 (1955), 67–71.

**[276] Rogers, E. M., "Technological Innovation in High Technology Industries," in *The Transfer and Utilization of Technical Knowledge*, ed. by D. Sahal. Lexington, Mass.: D. C. Heath, 1982.

**[277] Rogers, E. M., and F. Shoemaker, *Communication of Innovations: A Cross Cultural Approach*, 2nd ed., New York: Free Press of Glencoe, 1971.

[278] Rose, H., "The Conditions for Factor Augmenting Technical Change," *Econometrica*, **78 (1968), 966–971.

**[279] Rosegger, G., *The Economics of Production and Innovation*, Elmsford, N.Y.: Pergamon Press, 1980.

**[280] Rosenberg, N., *Technology and American Economic Growth*, Armonk, N.Y.: M. E. Sharpe, Inc., 1972.

*[281] Rothwell, R., "Some Indirect Impacts of Government Regulations of Industrial Innovation in the United States," *Technological Forecasting and Social Change*, **19** (1981), 57–80.

*[282] Rothwell, R., C. Freeman, A. Horsley, V. T. P. Jervis, A. B. Robertson, and J. Townsend, "SAPPHO Updated: Project SAPPHO, Phase II," *Research Policy*, **3** (1974), 258–291.

[283] Ruttan, V. W., "Usher and Schumpeter on Invention, Innovation, and Technological Change," *Quarterly Journal of Economics*, **73 (1959), 596–606.

[284] Rymes, T. K., "More on the Measurement of Total Factor Productivity," *Review of Income and Wealth*, **29 (1983), 297–316.

**[285] Sahal, D., *Patterns of Technological Innovation*, Reading, Mass.: Addison-Wesley, 1981.

[286] Sahal, D., "Foundations of Technometrics," *Technological Forecasting and Social Change*, **27 (1985), 1–37.

**[287] Salter, W. E. G., *Productivity and Technical Change*. Cambridge: The University Press, 1966.

[288] Samuelson, P., "A Theory of Induced Innovations Along Kennedy Weizsäcker Lines," *Review of Economics and Statistics*, **47 (1965), 343–356.

**[289] Sanders, B. S., "Some Difficulties in Measuring Inventive Activity," in *The Rate and Direction of Inventive Activity*, ed. by R. R. Nelson. Princeton: National Bureau of Economic Research, 1962.

*[290] Sato, R., "The Estimation of Biased Technical Progress and the Production Function," *International Economic Review*, **11** (1970), 179–208.

[291] Sato, R., "The Impact of Technical Change on the Holotheticity of Production Functions," *Review of Economic Studies*, **47 (1980), 767–776.

**[292] Sato, R., "R&D Activities and the Technology Game: A Dynamic Model of U.S.-Japan Competition," mimeo, 1984.

[293] Sato, R. and M. J. Beckmann, "Neutral Inventions and Production Functions," *Review of Economic Studies*, **35 (1968), 57–66.

**[294] Sato, R. and G. S. Suzawa: *Research and Productivity: Endogenous Technical Change*. Boston: Auburn House, 1983.

**[295] Schefold, B., "Fixed Capital as a Joint Product and the Analysis of Accumulation with Different Forms of Technical Progress," in *Essays on the Theory of Joint Production*, ed. by L. Pasinetti. New York: Columbia University Press, 1980.

[296] Scherer, F. M., "Firm Size, Market Structure, Opportunity and the Output of Patented Inventions," *American Economic Review*, **55 (1965), 1097–1125.

[297] Scherer, F. M., "Invention and Innovation in the Watt-Boulton Steam-Engine Venture," *Technology and Culture*, **6 (1965), 165–187.

**[298] Scherer, F. M., "Regulatory Dynamics and Economic Growth," in *Toward a New U.S. Industrial Policy?*, ed. by M. L. Wachter and S. M. Wachter. Philadelphia: University of Pennsylvania Press, 1981.

*[299] Scherer, F. M., "Inter-Industry Technology Flows and Productivity Growth," *Review of Economics and Statistics,* **6** (1982), 627–634.

*[300] Scherer, R. M., "Concentration, R&D, and Productivity Change," *Southern Economic Journal,* **50** (1983), 221–225.

*[301] Scherer, F. M., "The Propensity to Patent," *International Journal of Industrial Organization,* **1** (1983), 107–128.

*[302] Scherer, F. M., "R&D and Declining Productivity Growth," *American Economic Review,* **73** (1983), 215–218.

*[303] Scherer, F. M., "Using Linked Patent and R&D Data to Measure Inter-Industry Technology Flows," in *R&D, Patents, and Productivity,* ed. by Z. Griliches. Chicago: University of Chicago Press, 1984.

**[304] Scherer, F. M., "The World Productivity Growth Slump," in *Essays in Honor of Walter Goldberg,* ed. by R. Wolff, forthcoming.

**[305] Scherer, F. M., A. Beckenstein, E. Kaufer, R. D. Murphy, and F. Bougeon-Maassen, *The Economics of Multi-Plant Operation.* Cambridge, Mass.: Harvard University Press, 1975.

[306] Schmookler, J., "The Changing Efficiency of the American Economy, 1869–1938," *Review of Economics and Statistics,* **34 (1952), 214–231.

**[307] Schmookler, J., *Invention and Economic Growth.* Cambridge, Mass.: Harvard University Press, 1966.

**[308] Schultz, T. W., *The Economic Organization of Agriculture.* New York: McGraw-Hill, 1953.

[309] Schultz, T. W., "Investments in Entrepreneurial Ability," *Scandanavian Journal of Economics,* **82 (1980), 437–448.

**[310] Schumpeter, J. A., *The Theory of Economic Development.* Cambridge, Mass.: Harvard University Press, 1934.

**[311] Schumpeter, J. A., *Business Cycles.* New York: McGraw-Hill, 1939.

**[312] Science Policy Research Unit, *Success and Failure in Industrial Innovation.* University of Sussex: Center for the Study of Industrial Innovation, 1972.

**[313] Scott, J., "Firm versus Industry Variability in R&D Intensity," in *R&D, Patents, and Productivity,* ed. by Z. Griliches. Chicago: University of Chicago Press, 1984.

**[314] Siegel, R., "Why Has Productivity Slowed Down?" *Data Resources U.S. Review,* (1979), 59–65.

**[315] Smith, A., *An Inquiry into the Nature and Causes of the Wealth of Nations.* New York: Random House, 1937 [originally 1776].

[316] Smyth, D. J., J. M. Samuels, and J. Tzoannos, "Patents, Profitability, Liquidity and Firm Size," *Applied Economics,* **4 (1972), 77–86.

[317] Solow, R. M., "The Production Function and the Theory of Capital," *Review of Economic Studies,* **23 (1955), 101–108.

*[318] Solow, R. M., "Technical Change and the Aggregate Production Function," *Review of Economics and Statistics,* 39 (1957), 312–320.

**[319] Solow, R. M., "Investment and Technical Progress," in *Mathematical Methods in the Social Sciences, 1959,* ed. by K. J. Arrow et al. Stanford: Stanford University Press, 1960.

*[320] Solow, R. M., "Technical Progress, Capital Formation and Economic Growth," *American Economic Review,* **52** (1962), 76–86.

**[321] Solow, R. M., "Some Recent Developments in the Theory of Production," in *The Theory and Empirical Analysis of Production,* ed. by M. Brown. Princeton: National Bureau of Economic Research, 1967.

**[322] Solow, R. M., *Growth Theory: An Exposition.* New York: Oxford University Press, 1970.

[323] Star, S., "Accounting for Growth of Output," *American Economic Review*, **64 (1974), 123–135.

**[324] Stein, H., "Economic Problems of the Industrial Democracies: A View from the United States," *The AEI Economist*, (1981), 8–12.

**[325] Stigler, G. J., *Trends in Output and Employment*. New York: National Bureau of Economic Research, 1947.

**[326] Stigler, G. J., "Economic Problems in Measuring Changes in Productivity," in *Output, Input, and Productivity Measurement*. Princeton: National Bureau of Economic Research, 1961.

[327] Stokes, H. K. Jr., "An Examination of the Productivity Decline in the Construction Industry," *Review of Economics and Statistics*, **63 (1981), 495–502.

*[328] Stoneman, P., *The Economic Analysis of Technological Change*. Oxford: Oxford University Press, 1983.

**[329] Sudit, E. F. and N. Finger, "Methodological Issues in Aggregate Productivity Analysis," in *Aggregate and Industry-Level Productivity Analyses*, ed. by A. Dogramaci and N. R. Adam. Boston: Martinus Nijhoff, 1981.

[330] Suzuki, K., "Knowledge Capital and the Private Rate of Return to R&D in Japanese Manufacturing Industries," *International Journal of Industrial Organization*, **3 (1985), 293–305.

**[331] Sveikauskas, L., "Major Industrial Innovations: Research and Development and Productivity Growth," mimeo, 1984.

[332] Sveikauskas, C. D. and L. Sveikauskas, "Industry Characteristics and Productivity Growth," *Southern Economic Journal*, **48 (1982), 769–774.

[333] Switzer, L., "The Determinants of Industrial R&D: A Funds Flow Simultaneous Equation Approach," *Review of Economic and Statistics*, **66 (1984), 163–168.

[334] Sylos-Labini, P., "Factors Affecting Changes in Productivity," *Journal of Post-Keynesian Economics*, **6 (1983), 161–179.

*[335] Tassey, G., "Infratechnologies and the Role of Government," *Technological Forecasting and Social Change*, **21** (1982), 163–180.

[336] Tatom, J. A., "The Productivity Problem," *Economic Review of the Federal Reserve Bank of St. Louis*, **61 (1979), 3–16.

**[337] Terborgh, G., "A Quizzical Look at Productivity Statistics," *Capital Goods Review*, (1979), 1–4.

**[338] Terleckyj, N. E., "Sources of Productivity Advance: A Pilot Study of Manufacturing Industries 1899–1953," Ph.D. dissertation, Columbia University, 1960.

*[339] Terleckyj, N. E., *Effects of R&D on the Productivity Growth of Industries: An Exploratory Study*. Washington, D.C.: National Planning Association, 1974.

*[340] Terleckyj, N. E., "Direct and Indirect Effects of Industrial Research and Development on the Productivity Growth of Industries," in *New Developments in Productivity Measurement and Analysis*, ed. by J. W. Kendrick and B. N. Vaccara. Chicago: University of Chicago Press, 1980.

[341] Terleckyj, N. E., "What Do R&D Numbers Tell Us About Technological Change?" *American Economic Review*, **70 (1980), 55–61.

**[342] Terleckyj, N. E., "R&D and the U.S. Industrial Productivity in the 1970s," in *The Transfer and Utilization of Technological Knowledge*, ed. by D. Sahal, Lexington, Mass.: D. C. Heath, 1982.

**[343] Tinbergen, J., "On the Theory of Trend Movements," translated in *Jan*

Tinbergen, *Selected Papers*, ed. by L. H. Klassen, L. M. Koyck, and H. J. Witteveen. Amsterdam: North-Holland, 1959 [original paper in 1942].

**[344] Tornatzky, L. G., *The Process of Technological Innovation: Reviewing the Literature*. Washington, D.C.: National Science Foundation, 1983.

**[345] Usher, A. P., *A History of Mechanical Inventions*. Cambridge, Mass.: Harvard University Press, 1954.

[346] Utterback, J. M., and W. J. Abernathy, "A Dynamic Model of Process and Product Innovation," *Omega, The International Journal of Management Science*, **3 (1975), 639–656.

[347] Uzawa, H., "Neutral Inventions and the Stability of Growth Equilibrium," *Review of Economic Studies*, **28 (1961), 117–124.

[348] Valavanis-Vail, S., "An Econometric Model of Growth," *American Economic Review*, **45 (1955), 208–221.

[349] Verdoorn, P. J., "Verdoorn's Law in Retrospect: A Comment," *Economic Journal*, **90 (1980), 382–385.

[350] Von Weizsäcker, C., "Tentative Notes on a Two-Sector Model with Induced Technical Progress," *Review of Economic Studies*, **33 (1966), 245–251.

[351] Walters, A. A., "A Note on Economies of Scale," *Review of Economics and Statistics*, **45 (1963), 425–426.

[352] Walters, A. A., "Production and Cost Functions: An Econometric Survey," *Econometrica*, **31 (1963), 1–66.

[353] Weisskopf, T. E., S. Bowles, and D. M. Gordon, "Hearts and Minds: A Social Model of U.S. Productivity Growth," *Brookings Papers on Economic Activity*, **2 (1983), 381–441.

**[354] Weitzman, M. L., "Industrial Production," in *The Soviet Economy: Toward the Year 2000*, ed. by A. Bergson and H. S. Levine. London: Allen & Unwin, 1983.

[355] Westfield, F., "Technical Progress and Returns to Scale," *Review of Economics and Statistics*, **48 (1966), 432–441.

[356] Wickens, M., "Estimation of the Vintage Cobb-Douglas Production Function for the United States, 1900/1960," *Review of Economics and Statistics*, **52 (1970), 187–193.

**[357] Williamson, O. E., *Markets and Hierarchies: Analysis and Antitrust Implications*. New York: Free Press, 1975.

[358] Williamson, O. E., "Transaction-Cost Economics: The Governance of the Contractural Relations," *Journal of Law and Economics*, **22 (1979), 233–262.

**[359] Wolff, E., "Comments on Denison," in *International Comparisons of Productivity and Causes of the Slowdown*, ed. by J. W. Kendrick. Cambridge, Mass.: Ballinger, 1984.

**[360] Yamada, S., and V. W. Ruttan, "International Comparisons of Productivity in Agriculture," in *New Developments in Productivity Measurement and Analysis*, ed. by J. W. Kendrick and B. N. Vaccara. Chicago: University of Chicago Press, 1980.

**[361] Zaltman, G., R. Duncan, and J. Holbek, *Innovations and Organizations*. New York: John Wiley, 1973.

SUBJECT INDEX

FUNDAMENTALS OF PURE AND APPLIED ECONOMICS

Additional volumes in preparation
ISSN: 0191-1708